£9.99

Classes in Modern Society

Classes in Modern Society

Second edition

TOM BOTTOMORE

First published in 1991 by HarperCollins

Reprinted in 1992
by Routledge
11 New Fetter Lane, London EC4P 4EE

Simultaneously published in the USA and Canada
by Routledge
a division of Routledge, Chapman and Hall, Inc.
29 West 35th Street, New York, NY 10001

© Tom Bottomore 1991

Printed and bound in Great Britain by
Billing and Sons Limited, London and Worcester

British Library Cataloguing in Publication Data

A catalogue record for this book is available from the British
Library.

ISBN 0–415–08433–4

Contents

Preface

In 1955, when the original version of this book was published, the main elements of the post-war world had taken shape and social scientists were engaged in lively debate about the new forms of society which might eventually emerge from the economic and political upheavals of the first half of the twentieth century. Not the least of their concerns was the changing pattern of social inequality and its implications for future development. Was the class structure in capitalist countries being radically transformed, and were some of them moving towards a democratic socialist type of society, with the welfare state as a half-way house? Were the socialist countries, after the death of Stalin, really beginning to create a 'classless society', less totalitarian and oppressive in its political system? Were other kinds of inequality, associated with the formation of new élites, with gender, race or nationality, or with the vast difference in living standards between the industrially developed countries and the newly independent nations of the Third World, becoming more important?

In discussing these issues I concentrated on the problem of class, and argued that an adequate treatment of the subject required a thorough analysis of the historical development of the class structure in modern societies. My own projected study of classes in Europe and North America was never completed, for a variety of reasons, although I have used material from it in other writings; and since that period, from the mid-1950s to the mid-1960s, when I was most deeply involved in the study of classes and élites, profound changes have taken place in the world economy, and particularly in the major industrial countries, both capitalist and socialist.

Today there are new economic and political upheavals, and this is an opportune time to reconsider the questions that I posed, and my account of the processes at work, thirty-five years ago. However, the changes of the past two or three decades, and more particularly the recent dramatic events in the socialist countries of Eastern Europe, cannot be adequately studied in isolation. Hence I retain in the present edition much of my discussion of the historical development of capitalist societies from *laissez-faire* and the cycle of boom and depression to 'organized capitalism', characterized by partial planning, greatly increased public expenditure, and more stable economic growth; and of socialist societies from highly centralized planning and rapid industrial growth, through the era of political dictatorship and bureaucratic stagnation, to the experiments with 'market socialism'.

As in the previous edition I also go beyond a descriptive account of particular social classes, in two ways: first, by concentrating on the class structure – that is to say, the relations between classes in a specific type of social hierarchy – and, second, by examining the theoretical explanations that have been proposed for the constitution, perpetuation, modification or transformation of this hierarchical system. The starting point for this analysis is Marx's theory of class, which has had a central place in all modern research and controversy in this field; and in the present extended edition I go on to consider some recent criticisms and reformulations of the Marxist theory, as well as alternative conceptions of the social hierarchy suggested by Max Weber and the élite theorists.

In the concluding chapter I consider some of the main tendencies of development in present-day societies, within the limits imposed by the difficulties attending all sociological prognosis. The tendencies we observe may be compatible with more than one outcome, or they may encounter obstacles which prevent them from running their full course, as has certainly been the case with the egalitarian movements that began in the eighteenth century. These movements now operate in vastly changed conditions, and they have become more diverse, less pre-eminently class movements, than they were earlier in this century. Nevertheless, their vitality seems to me unimpaired, and, as I shall argue, classes play a more important part than is generally recognized by those who confine their attention to the working class and the middle class, while virtually ignoring the dominant role of the capitalist class in an international context. Here again it becomes evident that an adequate sociological analysis needs to deal with the class structure as a whole, not with isolated segments of it, and to trace carefully the long-term processes of structural change. It is from this standpoint that the present study is undertaken.

Introduction

The division of society into classes or strata ranged in a hierarchy of wealth, prestige and power is a prominent and almost universal feature of social structure which has always attracted the attention of social theorists and philosophers. During the greater part of human history these social inequalities have been largely accepted as an unalterable fact. Ancient and medieval writers, when they touched upon the subject of the social hierarchy, tended to provide a rationalization and justification of the established order, very often in terms of some religious doctrine concerning the origin of social ranks (as is apparent, for example, in the Hindu religious myths concerning the formation of the caste system). On the other side, the sporadic rebellions of the poor and oppressed were usually revolts against particularly irksome conditions rather than against the whole system of ranks, and they did not give rise to any clear conceptions of an alternative form of society.

Only in modern times, and particularly since the eighteenth century, has social class, as a stark embodiment of the principle of inequality, become an object of scientific enquiry, and at the same time of widespread condemnation in terms of new social doctrines. The revolutionary ideal of equality, however variously it came to be interpreted by nineteenth-century thinkers, at least implied an opposition to hereditary privileges and an immutable hierarchy of ranks; and the egalitarian movements slowly achieved an extension of civil and political rights and a greater degree of equality of opportunity. But at the same time the new post-feudal social order gave rise to a new hierarchy based directly upon the possession of wealth and economic power, and this in turn was attacked by socialist thinkers who believed that the ideal of equality ultimately implied a 'classless society'.

During the past hundred years great changes have taken place in the social structure of the advanced industrial countries.

The history of this period can be seen in part as a record of the growth of equality in new spheres of social life, or, as some writers have expressed it, of the growth of citizenship.[1] *Laissez-faire* capitalism – and especially the doctrine of *laissez-faire*, which was more extreme than the practice – has largely disappeared, in spite of a few vain attempts to restore it, and in all the industrial countries there is some degree of central economic planning, some attempt to regulate the distribution of wealth and income, and a more or less elaborate public provision of a wide range of social services. None the less, there are important differences between the two principal types of industrial society, the capitalist societies[2] of Western Europe, North America, Japan and South East Asia and the socialist societies[3] of Eastern Europe and elsewhere. In the former, there has been a gradual and limited movement towards 'classlessness', which is usually held to be especially marked in the period since the Second World War – the era of the welfare state – and has resulted from changes in the relative earnings of different occupational groups and in rates of taxation, from improvements in education and social services, from increasing opportunities for individual social mobility, and perhaps most of all from the sustained post-war growth of national income. The changes will be examined more closely in Chapter 2, but it is evident at once that they do not amount to an abolition of classes. These societies are still capitalist, and have a clearly delineated class structure, in the sense that their economic systems are dominated (though in differing degrees) by privately owned industrial and financial enterprises, and that immense economic and social differences exist between these property owners and a majority of the rest of the population.

In the socialist societies, on the other hand, the claim was made that social classes, or at least the hierarchical class structure, had disappeared with the abolition of private ownership of the means of production; and that the construction of a classless, socialist society was under way. This claim was not at first very closely examined, even by critics of Soviet society, who concentrated their attention during the Stalinist period upon more blatant features of the social system – the repression of personal freedom and the prevalence of coercion and terror.

Indeed, it seems to have been quite widely held at one time that the political dictatorship itself could be explained – in terms of an antithesis between liberty and equality – as a consequence of the attempt to enforce an 'unnatural' equality of condition upon the members of society. But this was seen to be implausible when it was realized that there were great social inequalities in these countries; and in later studies the discussion centred upon the emergence of a new 'ruling class', and upon comparisons between the characteristics of élite groups in capitalist and socialist societies.

It is the main purpose of this book to consider how the movement towards social equality which began with the eighteenth-century revolutions has affected the social hierarchy in the industrial societies, and how, in turn, it has been influenced by the development of modern industry. This calls, in the first place, for an enquiry into the nature of modern social classes. It requires, secondly, a comparative study of the changes in social stratification which have occurred in the two principal types of industrial society, and an attempt to explain these changes. Lastly, it involves a confrontation between the ideas of equality and social hierarchy. Is equality an attainable ideal in the circumstances of a complex industrial society? And, conversely, what kinds and degrees of inequality are inescapable, tolerable, or even desirable, in such a society?

These questions necessarily lead to a discussion of other kinds of inequality besides those embedded in the class structure, but I shall argue that class has a central importance and that its influence pervades the whole system of inequality. Further, I shall argue that there is no historical point at which a substantial degree of social equality – a body of equal rights and liberties – can be regarded as having been definitively and irrevocably established. The experience of socialist societies, and less blatantly of some capitalist societies, shows plainly that the movement towards greater equality can always be reversed, that new privileges, new élites and new forms of class structure can be created and consolidated by political power. We should learn from this that the price of equality, like that of its twin sister liberty, is eternal vigilance.

NOTES

1   See especially T. H. Marshall (1950).
2   I use the terms 'capitalism' and 'capitalist society' as they are
    habitually used by economic historians and sociologists, to refer
    to an economic and social system existing during a particular
    historical period, which is characterized principally by freedom of
    the market, free labour (i.e. individuals who are legally free and
    economically compelled to sell their labour power on the market),
    and private ownership of the means of production by industrial
    enterprises. These, together with secondary characteristics, make
    it possible to distinguish with reasonable clarity between capitalism
    and other types of society, such as feudalism or socialist society.
    This is not to say, however, that actual capitalist societies have
    remained unchanged since their origins, that there are not subtypes
    of capitalism, or that mixed and transitional forms of society cannot
    occur. Some of these questions will be discussed more fully later in
    this book. See also Bottomore (1985).
3   By 'socialist societies' I mean those societies in which the major
    means of production are publicly owned, though in various forms,
    and which have described themselves as socialist. Whether they
    were, or are, socialist in the broad sense of being egalitarian and
    classless is an issue to be examined in Chapter 3. They were
    certainly not democratic socialist societies during most of their
    history.

1
The Nature
of Social Class

There has always been much controversy among sociologists about the theory of social class, and, more generally, of social stratification. The latter term may be used to refer to any hierarchical ordering of social groups or strata in a society; sociologists have generally distinguished its principal forms as being those of slavery, caste, estate, social class, and status group. Each of these types of social stratification is complex, and there are many unsettled questions about the basis and characteristics of slavery, castes and estates,[1] just as there are about classes and status groups; even though the former are more easily defined, and their boundaries more clearly distinguishable, in most cases. In spite of these difficulties, there are some general features of social stratification which are not in dispute.

In the first place, a system of ranks does not form part of some natural and invariable order of things, but is a human contrivance or product, and is subject to historical changes. More particularly, natural or biological inequalities, on one side, and the distinctions of social rank on the other, belong to two distinct orders of fact. The differences were pointed out very clearly by Rousseau in a well-known passage:

I conceive that there are two kinds of inequality among the human species; one, which I call natural or physical, because it is established by nature, and consists in a difference of age, health, bodily strength, and the qualities of the mind or of the soul; and another, which may be called moral or political inequality, because it depends on a kind of convention, and is established, or at least authorized, by the consent of men.

This latter consists of the different privileges, which some men enjoy to the prejudice of others; such as that of being more rich, more honoured, more powerful, or even in a position to exact obedience.[2]

The distinction has been recognized by most modern writers on social class. Thus T. H. Marshall (1950, p. 115) observed that 'the institution of class teaches the members of a society to notice some differences and to ignore others when arranging persons in order of social merit'. It might be argued, however, while accepting this distinction, that the class system in modern capitalist societies does actually operate in such a way as to ensure a rough correspondence between the hierarchy of natural abilities and the socially recognized distinctions of rank. Such arguments have often been put forward, notably by the élite theorists whose ideas I have criticized elsewhere (Bottomore, 1964), but they are not well supported by the facts. It is generally admitted that the inequality of incomes is one important element in the class hierarchy. But numerous investigations have established that the inequality of incomes depends very largely upon the unequal distribution of property through inheritance, and not primarily upon the differences in earned income, which might be supposed to have some connection with natural, or innate, abilities.[3] Modern studies of educational and occupational selection underline this lack of correspondence between the hierarchies of ability and of social position, inasmuch as they make clear that intellectual ability, for example, is by no means always rewarded with high income or high social status, nor lack of ability with the opposite. Indeed, it would be a more accurate description of the class system to say that it operates (largely through the inheritance of property) to ensure that individuals maintain a certain social position, determined by their family situation and irrespective of their particular abilities. This state of affairs is only mitigated, not abolished, by various social influences which I shall consider later.

A second point of general agreement is that modern social classes, in contrast with castes or feudal estates, are more exclusively economic groups. They are not constituted or supported by any specific legal or religious rules, and membership in a particular social class generally confers upon the individual no special civil or political rights. It follows from this that the boundaries of social classes are less precisely defined. The principal classes – bourgeoisie and working class – may be fairly easily identifiable in most societies, but there are many intermediate strata, conveniently referred to as the 'middle class', the boundaries of which are difficult to state exactly, and membership in which cannot be determined in any simple fashion.

Furthermore, the membership of modern social classes is usually less stable than that of other types of hierarchical group. Individuals are born into a particular class, just as they are born into a caste or estate, but they are somewhat less likely to remain in their class of origin than are those in a caste or estate society. Within one generation, individuals or whole families may rise or fall in the social hierarchy. If they rise, they need no patent of nobility, no kind of official recognition, to confirm their new status. It will be enough to be wealthy, to have a particular economic and occupational role, and perhaps to acquire some of the secondary cultural characteristics of the social stratum into which they have moved.

While the economic basis of social classes is obvious, the fact may be interpreted in various ways, which gives rise to widely differing views of the relations between classes and their importance in the whole pattern of social life. It will be useful to begin an examination of this subject by considering Marx's theory of class, which affirms very strongly the economic basis of classes, the antagonistic relations between them, and their major role in social development. In principle, Marx's theory applies to the whole span of recorded history, as the well-known phrase in the *Communist Manifesto* vigorously asserts: 'The history of all hitherto existing society[4] is the history of class struggles.' In fact, Marx first of all adopted a notion of class which was widely employed by historians and social theorists (including the early socialists) at the time when he began his sociological enquiries, and he was then largely concerned to fit this notion into the wider framework of his theory of social change, and to use it in analysing the development of one particular social system, namely modern capitalism. He indicated this himself when he wrote, in an early letter, 'no credit is due to me for discovering the existence of classes in modern society, nor yet the struggle between them. Long before me bourgeois historians had described the historical development of this struggle of the classes and bourgeois economists the economic anatomy of the classes.'[5] Marx went on to explain his own contribution as having been to show that the existence of classes is bound up with particular historical phases in the development of production, and that the conflict of classes in the modern capitalist societies will lead to the victory of the working class and to the inauguration of a classless, socialist society.

The distinctive features of Marx's theory are, therefore, the conception of social classes in terms of the system of production, and the idea of social development through class conflict which is to culminate in a new type of society without classes. As Marx (1844) saw it, 'the whole of what is called world history is nothing but the creation of man himself by human labour'. Man produces (and reproduces) himself in a physical and in a cultural sense.

> In the social production which men carry on, they enter into definite relations that are indispensable, and independent of their will; these relations of production correspond to a definite stage of development of their material powers of production. The totality of these relations of production constitutes the economic structure of society – the real foundation upon which legal and political superstructures arise and to which definite forms of social consciousness correspond. The mode of production of material life determines the general character of the social, political and spiritual processes of life. (1859, Preface)

Social classes originated with the first historical expansion of productive forces beyond the level needed for mere subsistence. The extension of the division of labour outside the family, the accumulation of surplus wealth, and the emergence of privately owned instruments of production formed the basis for the constitution of social classes. Marx distinguished several important epochs, or major forms of social structure, in the history of humanity: 'In broad outline we can designate the Asiatic, the ancient, the feudal, and the modern bourgeois modes of production as epochs in the progress of the economic formation of society' (1859, Preface). Elsewhere, he and Engels refer to primitive communism, ancient society (slavery), feudal society (serfdom), and modern capitalism (wage labour) as the principal historical forms of society. Marx's references to the Asiatic type of society are especially interesting because this lies outside the line of development of the Western societies, and also because he seems to accept the possibility that in this case a ruling class might be formed by the high officials who control the administration. But this theme, which presents several difficulties (Turner, 1983), was not pursued in his later work.

The historical changes from one type of society to another are brought about by class struggles and by the victory of one class over others. Class conflict itself reflects the incompatibility between different modes of production; and the victory of a particular class, as well as its subsequent reorganization of society, is conditional upon the emergence of a new and superior mode of production, which it is the interest of this class to establish as dominant. In Marx's words: 'No social order ever disappears before all the productive forces for which there is room in it have been developed; and new, higher relations of production never appear before the material conditions of their existence have matured in the womb of the old society' (1859, Preface).

Marx was not, however, expounding a simple theory of technological or economic determinism. On the contrary, as he asserted in his criticism of Hegel's philosophy of history: 'It is not "history" which uses men as a means of achieving – as if it were an individual person – *its* own ends. History is *nothing* but the activity of men in pursuit of their ends' (1845). Marx held very strongly (and his own intellectual and political activities would otherwise have been absurd) that the victory of a rising class depends upon its awareness of its situation and aims, and upon the effectiveness of its political organization, as well as upon its actual economic position. This is especially the case with the working class in capitalist society, and Marx discussed on several occasions the factors which might influence the development of its class consciousness and of its political maturity. In *The Poverty of Philosophy*, for example, he examined at some length the development of the working class, and added some critical remarks on the lack of empirical studies devoted to this most significant social movement:

> Many researches have been undertaken to trace the histori-
> cal stages through which the bourgeoisie passed, from the
> commune up to its constitution as a class. But when it is
> a question of gaining a clear understanding of the strikes,
> combinations, and other forms in which the proletarians are
> achieving, before our eyes, their organization as a class,
> some are seized with genuine fear, while others display a
> transcendental disdain. (1847)

It is one of the most important features of Marx's theory of class, therefore, that it attempts to take account of the interplay between the real situation of individuals in the process of production, on one side, and the conceptions which they form of their situation and of the lines of social and political action which are open to them, on the other; and in its application to modern societies the theory allows a very great influence to ideas and doctrines. Marx's conviction that the working class would be victorious within a relatively short space of time in its struggle against the bourgeoisie was founded largely upon his conclusion that modern large-scale factory production would be extremely favourable to the development of class consciousness, to the diffusion of socialist ideas, and to the organization of a political movement.

Like other nineteenth-century thinkers who contributed to the foundation of sociology, Marx was above all concerned to investigate the origins and development of modern capitalist society; he chose to do so largely in a single country – England – because it was at that time the most advanced industrial country, showing to others, as Marx claimed, 'the image of their own future'. But even in the case of modern society Marx did not set out his conception of class in a systematic form, and the observations scattered through his writings contain diverse and partially incompatible elements of a general theory. In particular, the assertion in the *Communist Manifesto* that

society is more and more splitting into two great classes, two
hostile camps, is heavily qualified in later writings. Thus, in the
incomplete fragment on social classes which Engels included in
the third volume of *Capital*, Marx observed that even in the
most developed capitalist country, England, 'intermediate and
transitional strata obscure the class boundaries'; and in two
passages in the manuscript of *Theories of Surplus Value* he
referred explicitly to the increase in numbers of the middle
class, saying that it is the 'trend of bourgeois society' that 'the
middle class will grow in size and the working class will form
a continually diminishing proportion of the total population'
(Bottomore, 1988, p. 19). Finally, in the *Grundrisse* Marx
seemed to envisage the creation of a new form of society
as resulting from the gradual substitution of knowledge for
human labour as the major productive force, but the nature
of the social conflict which would bring about a breakdown of
capitalism and a transition to socialism then becomes unclear
(Bottomore, 1988, pp. 19–21).

It was in its application to capitalist society in the mid-
nineteenth century that Marx's original conception of the modern class structure was most convincing. The course of industrial
development seemed to confirm the thesis that society was
becoming more clearly divided into two principal classes, a
small class of increasingly wealthy capitalists and a growing
mass of propertyless and impoverished wage-earners; and that
the social gulf between them was widening as a result of the
decline of the middle class (by which Marx meant the small
independent producers and the professions), whose members
were being transformed into dependent employees. At the
same time, the rise of the labour movement (of trade unions,
co-operatives, and socialist political parties) and the outbreak
of revolutionary conflicts all over Europe, especially in the years
up to 1848, provided evidence for Marx's prediction of a growth
of class consciousness in the working class, and its expression in
new social doctrines and new forms of political organization.

By the end of the nineteenth century, Marxism, as a social
theory and a political doctrine, was widely known and influential, above all in the rapidly growing socialist movement,
but also increasingly in the academic world.[6] The theory then

began to be critically discussed in the light of the development of capitalist societies since Marx's day, mainly by the opponents of socialism, but also among Marxists themselves. In the latter case the theory of class became a contentious issue in the 'revisionist debate' initiated by Bernstein (1899), who argued that the polarization of classes anticipated by Marx was not occurring, the concentration of capital in large enterprises was accompanied by a development of new small- and medium-size businesses, property ownership was becoming more widespread, the general standard of living was rising, the middle class was increasing rather than diminishing in number, and the structure of capitalist society was not being simplified but was becoming more complex and differentiated.[7] These themes, as we shall see, have remained prominent in all subsequent controversies, in the studies by Marxists as well as by their opponents,[8] while new issues have been raised by still later developments in the capitalist economy and the capitalist state.

One of the most important issues concerns the growth of a sense of national community and the influence of nationalism in modern nation states, which can be considered from two aspects. First, the extension of political and social rights to the whole population in the advanced capitalist countries has created a condition of 'citizenship' which, it may be argued, overcomes the division into 'two nations' and moderates, if it does not extinguish, the conflict between classes. Secondly, nationalism, in the twentieth century, has proved to be an immensely powerful force not only in the internal politics of modern nations but in the relations between them; and Marxists, it is said, have consistently underestimated it as a social force. This, however, is not entirely true, since the Austro-Marxists, confronted by nationalist movements in the multi-national Habsburg empire, devoted particular attention to it, and Bauer (1907) published what is still the outstanding Marxist study of the subject. Furthermore, Hilferding (1910), Adler (1915) and Renner (1917), as well as Bauer, all observed the transformation of nationalism into a new ideology of world domination in the age of imperialism,[9] and opposed socialism to nationalism in this form. However, the great strength of nationalism was shown by the inability of the socialist movement in

Western Europe to counter effectively the wave of nationalist sentiment in the First World War, or subsequently during the rise of fascism; and, more recently, nationalism, sometimes in association with religious movements, has been a powerful influence both in international politics and within existing states, more particularly those which are multi-national.

The question of class as a community versus the nation as a community thus remains a focus of controversy, and I shall return to other aspects of it later. The central issues concerning classes themselves, in the modern capitalist societies,[10] were initially formulated by Bernstein, and we have next to consider the further changes that have taken place in the class structure during the twentieth century. In broad outline, Marx predicted that the social gulf between the two principal classes, bourgeoisie and proletariat, would become wider, in part because of the increasing disparity between their conditions of life,[11] and in part because of the elimination of the intermediate strata of the population; that the class consciousness of the proletariat would develop and would assume a revolutionary character; and that the rule of the bourgeoisie would finally be overthrown by a revolution of the immense majority of the population.

Against this view numerous arguments have been presented, based upon sociological observation of the changes in the structure of modern societies. It is claimed, in the first place, that the gulf between bourgeoisie and proletariat has not widened, for several reasons. The productivity of modern industry, especially in the last few decades, has increased so greatly as to produce a considerable improvement in the general standard of living; and, even if the distribution of income between the classes had remained unchanged, this would still have raised working-class living standards to a point at which new aspirations and new social attitudes would be encouraged, far removed from those which support revolutionary aims. It is argued further, however, that the distribution of national income has actually changed in favour of the working class, thus reinforcing these tendencies. The extent of the redistribution of income and wealth in modern societies is a subject of controversy, and some of the relevant studies will be considered in the next chapter; but even a modest redistribution, together with the general rise in incomes, the expansion of social services, and greater security of employment, would clearly bring about an important change in the position of the working class in society. It is no longer possible in the late twentieth century to regard the working class in the advanced capitalist countries as being totally alienated from society, or, in Marx's phrase, as 'a class *in* civil society which is not a class *of* civil society'.

Another change which presents difficulties for Marx's theory is the growth of the 'new middle class', as a result of economic development. This does not directly falsify Marx's argument in his earlier writings that the middle class would gradually disappear from capitalist societies, because he was there referring to the large numbers of small producers, craftsmen, artisans, small farmers, and self-employed professional people, many of whom were in fact absorbed as paid employees into large capitalist enterprises. But it does contradict the view expressed in the *Communist Manifesto* that the 'intermediate strata' as such were tending to disappear, and that the bourgeois epoch had as its distinctive feature that class antagonisms had been simplified, and society was splitting up more and more into two great hostile camps. The rapid growth of the new middle class – comprising office workers, supervisors, managers, scientists, and many of those who are employed in providing services of one kind or another (in social welfare, entertainment, leisure activities) – has produced a greater complexity of social stratification in capitalist society, introducing or reintroducing as an important element of stratification, alongside class divisions, social prestige based upon occupation, consumption and style of life.

Marx himself recognized in later writings the growth of the middle class, which he described as the 'trend of bourgeois society', and a transformation of the economy, as a result of the rapid progress of science and technology, from one based upon labour to one based upon knowledge (see above, page 11), but he did not explore the political implications of these developments. Later Marxists, beginning with Bernstein, were obliged to study such phenomena more closely, in the context of the difficulties experienced by socialist parties in gaining the support of a majority of the population. Hilferding (1910,

p. 347) noted that the growth of salaried employment had created a new hierarchical system which helps to sustain the bourgeois social order: 'The interest in a career, the drive for advancement which develops in every hierarchy, is thus kindled in each individual employee and triumphs over his feelings of solidarity. Everyone hopes to rise above the others and to work his way out of his semi-proletarian condition to the heights of capitalist income.' In his last unfinished work, after the experience of the rise of fascism, Hilferding returned to the problem of classes and argued that 'an analysis which differentiates along economic lines tends only too readily to subsume all the interests which are active in society under the interests of the basic economic classes; it thus fails to meet the requirements of historical analysis, and perhaps also of political analysis' (1941, translated in Bottomore, 1988, p. 120). Other Marxists similarly recognized the increasing complexity of the class structure, and the diversity of interest groups, in modern capitalist society.[12]

But the most direct challenge to the original Marxist theory came from Max Weber (1921, in Gerth and Mills, 1947, pp. 180–95), in the distinction he made between class stratification and stratification by social prestige or honour. In his conception it is clear that stratification by prestige, which gives rise to the formation of status groups, is regarded as having its source in those pre-capitalist groups which enjoyed social honour, such as the various sections of the nobility, the scholarly professions, and the high officials; but the new middle class in the advanced industrial societies exhibits some at least of the same features in basing its claims to social position upon educational and cultural characteristics, the nature of its occupations, and its particular styles of life.

Stratification by prestige affects the class system, as Marx conceived it, in two important ways: first, by interposing between the two major classes a range of status groups which bridge the gulf between the extreme positions in the class structure; and, secondly, by suggesting an entirely different conception of the social hierarchy as a whole, according to which it appears as a continuum of more or less clearly defined status positions, determined by a variety of factors and not simply by property ownership, which is incompatible with the formation of massive social classes and with the existence of a fundamental conflict between classes. The relations between status groups at different levels are relations of competition and emulation, not of conflict. With the growth in numbers of the middle class, which forms an increasing proportion of the whole population, this view of the social hierarchy as a continuum of prestige ranks (or statuses) without any sharp breaks, and thus without any clear lines of conflict between major social groups, has acquired a much greater influence upon social thought, and its diffusion has been one factor limiting the development of class consciousness. Consequently, whereas Weber regarded class stratification and status stratification as coexisting in modern capitalist societies (their relative importance fluctuating with changes in technology and economic conditions), some more recent sociologists concluded that status groups have now become far more important than social classes in the system of stratification as a whole.

This conclusion is supported by two other arguments. One of them asserts that the amount of social mobility in industrial societies is so considerable as to prevent the consolidation and persistence of classes in Marx's sense, and that, on the contrary, it too makes plausible the image of the social hierarchy as a series of levels of prestige, as a ladder with closely adjacent rungs, which individuals may climb or descend according to their capacities.[13] However, the amount and range of social mobility, like the distribution of income, have been assessed in conflicting ways, and some of the evidence from recent studies will be considered later.

A second argument is derived from the distinction which Weber made between the distribution of political power, as an independent phenomenon, and social stratification by class or by status.[14] This distinction was later formulated in strong terms by Dahrendorf (1959), who argued that the coincidence of economic conflict and political conflict, which was the foundation of Marx's theory, had ceased to exist in what he termed the 'post-capitalist societies'. In capitalist society,

> the lines of industrial and political conflict were superimposed. The opponents of industry – capital and labour –

met again, as bourgeoisie and proletariat, in the political arena. . . . It is one of the central theses of the present analysis that in post-capitalist society, industry and society have, by contrast to capitalist society, been dissociated. Increasingly, the social relations of industry, including industrial conflict, do not dominate the whole of society but remain confined in their patterns and problems to the sphere of industry. Industry and industrial conflict are, in post-capitalist society, institutionally isolated, i.e. confined within the borders of their proper realm and robbed of their influence on other spheres of society. (1959, p. 268)

Raymond Aron (1950) had expounded a similar conception, radically qualifying the Marxist theory by ideas derived from the theory of élites (which will be discussed later). 'Inequality in political power', he argued, 'is in no way eliminated or diminished by the abolition of classes, for it is quite impossible for the government of a society to be in the hands of any but a few' (p. 135), and in terms of this argument he proposed to replace the Marxist theory of class rule and class conflict by the conception of a dominant élite and the struggles for political power between élites, in both capitalist and socialist societies.

Considered empirically, however, in relation to the capitalist countries, these arguments are more easily refuted than those of Marx which they are intended to replace, for numerous studies have shown that in Europe, and to a lesser extent in North America, major political conflicts have been closely and continuously associated with industrial conflicts and have expressed the divergent interests of the principal social classes. The kind of criticism of Marxist theory that I have just considered is more plausible in a less extreme formulation; as for example that there are other conflicting groups in society besides social classes, which may at times acquire great importance, that the association between industrial conflict and political conflict cannot simply be assumed, but must be investigated in each case, and that, with the development of the capitalist industrial societies, significant changes have occurred in the nature of political conflicts themselves which could not be clearly foreseen or taken into account by Marx.

Associated with these arguments against the Marxist view of class relations are others which question the analysis of the two major classes – bourgeoisie and proletariat – in the changed economic and social conditions of the twentieth century, and particularly since the Second World War. The bourgeoisie, it is argued, is no longer a closed, cohesive and enduring group. Its structure, composition, and stability over time have all been profoundly modified by the wider diffusion of property ownership and the breakup of large fortunes, by increasing social mobility, and by other changes in society. Furthermore, it can no longer be maintained that the bourgeoisie is a *ruling* class – first, because it has ceased to be a cohesive group; secondly, because the complexity and differentiation of modern societies make it difficult for any single group to wield power alone; and, finally, because democratic regimes ensure that political power is ultimately in the hands of the mass of the people. But these arguments, which rest upon far less research than has been devoted to the middle class or the working class, are far from convincing. When the available data are brought together it can easily be shown that inherited family wealth and ownership of productive resources still play a dominant part in capitalist societies, and that an identifiable class exists which also has immense political influence because of its possession of economic resources and its capacity, as an 'organized minority', to act in a coherent and effective way.[15]

It is, however, the changing circumstances of the working class that have been the main ground of criticism of the Marxist theory. Marx, in most of his writings (but with the qualifications that I noted earlier, page 11), anticipated a process of development in which the working class would become more homogeneous, because differences of skill and earnings would be reduced, if not obliterated, by the more extensive use of machinery; would become numerically stronger, because many members of the old middle class would sink to the condition of wage-earners; would become more united and class conscious as a result of the increasing similarity of conditions of life and work, the facility of communication among working-class organizations, and the spread of socialist doctrines; and, finally, would become a revolutionary force, because of the growing disparity between its own material conditions and those of the bourgeoisie, and the realization that only a radical transformation of society could make possible a tolerable human life for the great majority of people. Against this conception, critics have pointed out that the modern working class remains highly differentiated in respect of levels of skill, even though differences in earnings have tended to diminish; that increasing specialization of occupations has created a far more complex status system, as well as a multiplicity of sectional interests; that the expansion of the middle class has reduced the proportion of industrial workers in the total population and thereby diminished their social influence; that greater social mobility has undermined the solidarity of the working class; and that the general improvement in levels of living has brought about an embourgeoisement of large sections of the working class, which increasingly adopt middle-class standards and styles of life.

Some part of this criticism has certainly to be accepted in any realistic account of the working class in present-day capitalist societies (and was accepted by many Marxist social scientists from the end of the nineteenth century, as I have shown), but the changes which have taken place are still open to various interpretations. One particularly disputed thesis is that concerning the embourgeoisement of the working class, which has often been presented in a superficial and facile manner. A study by Goldthorpe and Lockwood (1963) observed that, as a result of recent studies of British society,

a picture has been built up – and it is one which would be generally accepted – of a system of stratification becoming increasingly fine in its gradations and at the same time somewhat less extreme and less rigid. Of late, however, still further economic progress has resulted in a new factor entering into the discussion – that of working class 'affluence' . . . . It has been argued by a number of writers that the working class, or at least a more prosperous section of it, is losing its identity as a social stratum and is becoming merged into the middle class. . . . This, one should note, is to claim a far more rapid and far-reaching change in class structure than any which could ensue from secular trends in occupational distribution, in the overall distribution of income and wealth or in rates of intergenerational social mobility. (p. 124)

The authors then distinguish and examine what they call the economic, the relational, and the normative aspects of the changes in working-class life. They point out that the economic progress of the working class in relation to the middle class has been exaggerated in many studies, because these do not take account of all the relevant factors, such as economic security, opportunities for promotion, and fringe benefits of various kinds. The other aspects, the relational (i.e. the extent to which manual workers are accepted on terms of equality by middle-class people in formal and informal social relationships) and the normative (i.e. the extent to which manual workers have acquired a new outlook and new standards of behaviour which resemble those of the middle class), have hardly been studied at all; but such evidence as there is suggests that the gulf between working class and middle class remains very wide. It follows that the political conclusions – the end of ideology and of class conflict – drawn from the so-called embourgeoisement of the working class, or, in other words, from the view that the modern capitalist countries are now middle-class societies, are themselves extremely dubious.

A study by Serge Mallet (1975) pointed to some conclusions supplementing those reached by Goldthorpe and Lockwood. Mallet made an important distinction between the situation of the worker in the spheres of consumption and of production. In the former, 'the working class has ceased to live apart. Its level of living and its aspirations for material comfort have led it out of the ghetto in which it was confined at the beginning of industrialization. The worker ceases to regard himself as a worker when he leaves the factory.' In the process of production itself, in contrast, 'the fundamental characteristics which distinguish the working class from other social strata seem to have remained unchanged' (p. 9). It is in industry, through the factory organizations and the trade unions, that the distinctive characteristics and outlook of the working class are maintained or changed; and Mallet argued, from his studies of three industrial enterprises, that the 'new working class' has been led, as a result of technological and economic changes, to assume greater responsibility for the organization of production, through its trade union representatives, and thus to see itself still, and perhaps even more clearly, as the eventual controller of industry in place of the present capitalist owners.

The development of capitalism throughout the post-war period – characterized (as compared with the 1920s and 1930s) by greater stability, greatly increased public expenditure, and high rates of economic growth, even though there are still cyclical fluctuations and in the 1980s a substantial recession which has placed new strains on 'welfare capitalism' – has tended to support the thesis that radical changes in the class structure have taken place; and in the past two decades there have again been numerous revisions of Marxist theory, along with a further elaboration of alternative theoretical schemes. Among those who can be broadly described as Marxists the variety of new approaches has been such that it is increasingly difficult to identify a central and distinctive body of thought. The social scientists influenced by Soviet Marxism generally retained a more or less traditional theory, still partly Stalinist in orientation, and largely out of touch with the development of both capitalist and socialist societies, but this has now finally disintegrated and will have no place in future Marxist thought. Western Marxists, for their part, have continued to analyse in diverse ways the problems posed by the changes in the working class and the middle class,[16] but have paid less attention to those in the capitalist class or to the nature of its persisting dominance. Some, like the Frankfurt School thinkers (Bottomore, 1984a), became increasingly sceptical about the political role of the working class in capitalist society, and ended with a scarcely recognizable form of 'Marxism without the proletariat' (Kolakowski, 1978, vol. III, p. 355). In their later writings, especially those of Marcuse (1964), as in the studies by some 'dependency theorists' (Larrain, 1989, ch. 4), Marx's conception of the class structure of capitalism was to some extent replaced by a theoretical scheme in which the main division is that between 'bourgeois' and 'proletarian' nations. The Frankfurt School thinkers also virtually abandoned Marx's analysis of capitalism as a form of society, substituting for it a conception of modern 'technological' society which is dominated, not by a capitalist class, but by the forces of scientific and technological progress. Subsequently, however, the study of classes, and of political power in relation to classes, was reintroduced by social theorists whose work derives, with many modifications, from the 'critical theory' of the Frankfurt School (Habermas, 1973; Offe, 1972), although this still has a limited place in their analysis.

Other Western Marxists have dealt more directly with the problems of class structure in their revisions of Marxist theory. Poulantzas (1968, 1974) set out to construct a more rigorous model of classes and political power, but his structuralist approach (derived from Althusser's conception of Marxism as a science) soon revealed a number of weaknesses. It concentrates on theoretical models and pays little attention to empirical confirmation of the propositions derived from them; it conflates class, class consciousness, and political organization, thereby obscuring all the problems of the historically changing relationship between them and excluding any influence of conscious action and particular historical circumstances on the course of class struggles or on the diverse forms of the capitalist state; and by its very restrictive definition of the working class reduces this to a small minority of the population in advanced capitalist countries, thus exacerbating the difficulties that exist for Marxist conceptions of political change and a transition to socialism.

A quite different approach is suggested by Roemer (1982) and Wright (1985), who propose a new framework for the analysis of class, based on the general concept of exploitation within a determinate system of property relations. This extends, rather than narrowing, the boundaries of a subordinate class or classes, but by substituting property relations in general for relations of production as a central concept it loses the sharpness of definition of classes, and especially the capitalist class, which characterizes Marx's theory. Wright goes on to analyse as a distinctive feature of the middle class the existence of contradictory class locations for many of its members, though this has long been recognized in one way or another by Marxists, and the most important question remains the changing political allegiances of particular sections of the middle class in various historical circumstances. Wright does in fact consider this question in another context when he makes a comparison between the working class in Sweden and in the United States, and concludes that 'the level of working class consciousness in a given society and the nature of the class coalitions . . . are shaped by the organizational and political practices that characterize the history of class struggle' (1985, p. 278).

The criticisms and revisions of Marxist theory that I have considered so far arise from the growing complexity of stratification, changes in the position of various classes, variations in economic and social conditions, the changing role of the state, and the emergence of new political concerns and allegiances, in capitalist societies. But there is another major strand in the criticism of Marxism which became increasingly important after the Second World War and acquired exceptional prominence in the late 1980s in the course of a dramatic reconstruction of socialist societies in Eastern Europe. It was an essential element of Marx's theory of class that he conceived capitalism as 'the last antagonistic form of society', following which, with the rise to dominance of the working class, a society without classes would be inaugurated. Neither Marx nor the first generation of Marxists provided much in the way of a precise and detailed outline of the economic or political institutions of this new society, and Marx on one or two occasions used the ill-fated expression 'dictatorship of the proletariat',[17] but there is no doubt that they conceived socialism as a liberated society in which the mass of people would become, to the largest possible extent, self-governing, and the autocratic powers of the state would be drastically curtailed.

The reality turned out to be very different. In the Soviet Union tendencies towards political dictatorship (responding in part, it is true, to the conditions of civil war and foreign intervention) appeared at an early stage, and were vigorously criticized by many Marxists, among them Rosa Luxemburg, Kautsky, the Austro-Marxists, and Alexandra Kollontai, who was an active member of the Workers' Opposition inside the Soviet Union. These tendencies finally matured in Stalin's dictatorship, which was then imposed upon the countries of Eastern Europe after 1945, succeeded by neo-Stalinist regimes that only began to be swept away in the late 1980s. As I have indicated, these developments were criticized from the beginning by many Marxists (though many others, in the communist parties, tenaciously defended them until recent years), but the critics either did not explain at all, or explained in very diverse ways, how such conditions could arise out of political movements and revolutions which aimed to liberate humanity. Increasingly, therefore, alternative conceptions of stratification and political power, derived from Max Weber and the élite theorists, gained a more prominent place in the analysis of both advanced capitalist and socialist societies.

The debates among Marxists have centred mainly on the question whether a new ruling class emerged in the Soviet Union and subsequently in other socialist countries. Among those who argued that a new class was being formed, or had been formed, Djilas (1957, p. 39) maintained that Communist Party officials constituted a ruling class 'made up of those who have special privileges and economic preference because of the administrative monopoly they hold', while Konrád and Szelényi (1979, p. 145) defined the 'social structure of early socialism' as a class structure, 'and indeed a dichotomous one. . . . At one pole is an evolving class of intellectuals who occupy the position of redistributors, at the other a working class which produces the social surplus but has no right of disposition over it', though they also recognized that, as in the capitalist societies, 'an ever larger fraction of the population must be assigned to the intermediate strata'. Trotsky (1937), on the other hand, rejected the idea of a new class and characterized the bureaucracy as the 'ruling group' in a 'degenerated workers' state', though he recognized as one possibility its metamorphosis into a new bourgeoisie.

Other critics, however, emphasized most strongly the role of the state in creating a new social hierarchy. Hilferding (1940, 1941) argued that 'the subjection of the economy by the holders of state power' had created a totalitarian state economy, and Ossowski (1963, p. 184), referring primarily to the socialist countries of Eastern Europe, observed:

In situations where changes of social structure are to a greater or lesser extent governed by the decision of the political authorities, we are a long way from social class as interpreted by Marx, Ward, Veblen or Weber, from classes conceived of as groups determined by their relations to the means of production or, as others would say, by their relations to the market. We are a long way from classes conceived of as groups arising out of the spontaneously created class organizations. In situations where the political authorities can overtly and effectively change the class structure; where the privileges that are most essential for social status, including that of a higher share in the national income, are conferred by a decision of the political authorities; where a large part or even the majority of the population is included in a stratification of the type to be found in a bureaucratic hierarchy – the nineteenth-century concept of class becomes more or less an anachronism, and class conflicts give way to other forms of social antagonism.

These critical studies of socialist societies have undoubtedly some affinities with non-Marxist analyses of the social hierarchy, and particularly with those of Max Weber and the élite theorists, which became, in several respects, more influential. Weber's (1918) well-known observation that a transition to socialism would be more likely to establish the 'dictatorship of the official' than the 'dictatorship of the proletariat' has an obvious relevance to the actual development of socialist societies, and his general conception of the nature of social stratification (Weber, 1921) also has a wider application to both capitalist and socialist societies. In the first place, his distinction between classes and status groups makes possible a more refined analysis of the complexities of stratification in modern societies. It has been widely, though diversely, used in studies of the middle class,[18] although at times conceived in such a way as to bring all the phenomena of stratification within the compass of a theory of status groups in what were taken to be 'middle-class societies' in the capitalist world. Weber himself retained the concepts of class *and* status, and argued that while classes are not communities they do 'represent possible, and frequent, bases for communal action'. However, he defined class only partly in a Marxist sense in terms of possession or non-possession of productive property (i.e. capital), and in a more general sense regarded class situation as being determined by market situation. Hence, although 'property' and 'lack of property' are 'the basic categories of all class situations', the variety of kinds of property that are 'usable for returns' differentiates in significant ways the class situations of the propertied.[19]

On the other hand, status groups, according to Weber, 'are normally communities', though often amorphous, characterized by a specific 'style of life', and determined by social estimations of 'honour' or 'prestige'. But they are closely linked with class situation, and Weber observed that, while 'property as such is not always recognized as a status qualification, in the long run it is, and with extraordinary regularity'. In broad terms the distinction between class and status can be expressed by saying that, whereas 'classes are stratified according to their relations to the production and acquisition of goods, status groups are stratified according to the principle of their consumption of goods'; but the two are nevertheless closely connected. Furthermore, the predominance of one or the other type of stratification in society as a whole is influenced by general economic conditions, and Weber suggests that 'when the bases of the acquisition and distribution of goods are relatively stable, stratification by status is favoured', but 'every technological repercussion and economic transformation threatens stratification by status and pushes the class situation into the foreground'.

Weber conceived classes, status groups, and parties as being all 'phenomena of the distribution of power within a community', but he made a distinction between stratification and political power.

> [Parties] need be neither purely 'class' nor purely 'status' parties. In most cases they are partly class parties, and partly status parties, but sometimes they are neither. They may represent ephemeral or enduring structures. Their means of attaining power may be quite varied, ranging from naked violence of any sort to canvassing for votes with coarse or

subtle means. . . (Weber 1921, cited from Gerth and Mills 1947, p. 194)

In his writings on German politics, Weber (1918, and other essays, 1971) expressed various conceptions of political power, emphasizing the power position of the bureaucracy, but maintaining generally that the entrepreneurial bourgeoisie was most capable, in principle, of providing effective political leadership, and rejecting the idea that the working class, through the Social Democratic Party, could do so. All Weber's political analysis is written explicitly from a nationalist standpoint, and is concerned with the choice of leaders who would effectively promote the interests of the nation state (Bottomore, 1984b, ch. 7). In this respect his conception of stratification and political power has affinities with the ideas of the élite theorists.

The theory of élites, as I have argued elsewhere (Bottomore, 1964), was developed, primarily by Pareto and Mosca, in direct opposition to the Marxist conception of a ruling class. First, it asserted that the division of society into dominant and subordinate groups is a universal and unalterable fact (Mosca, 1896, p. 50), and, secondly, it defined the ruling group in quite a different way – Pareto mainly in terms of the superior qualities of some individuals which produce élites in every sphere of life, Mosca in terms of the inevitable dominion of an 'organized minority' or 'political class' over the unorganized majority, though he also referred to the very influential personal attributes of this minority. But Mosca introduced many qualifications and eventually outlined a more complex theory (closer to Marxism) in which the political class itself is influenced and restrained by various 'social forces' and is connected with a large sub-élite comprising sections of the middle class, which is a vital element in ensuring political stability (Albertoni, 1987).

The élite theories influenced much of the later discussion of stratification and political power. Michels (1911), drawing upon the ideas of Pareto, Mosca, and Weber, formulated his 'iron law of oligarchy', according to which the leaders of parties (including socialist parties) and classes necessarily come to constitute a dominant élite, and subsequently greeted Mussolini as a model of the 'charismatic leader' proposed by Weber. Two major sociologists who later adopted a large part of élite theory, and were strongly influenced by Weber's concept of power, were Mills and Aron. Mills (1956) substituted the term 'power élite' for 'ruling class', because the latter did not allow enough autonomy to the political order, while Aron (1950) tried to establish a synthesis between Marxist ideas and those of Pareto, arguing that 'a society cannot be characterized only by the class which owns the means of production or by the psychological and social nature of the élite' (though it should be noted that some elements of such a synthesis were already present in the work of Mosca). Aron made particular use of the élite concept in contrasting the 'unified élite' in socialist societies with the plurality of élites in democratic capitalist societies, and later (1964, chs 9 and 10) he argued that the members of the ruling group in Soviet society have 'infinitely more power than the political rulers in a democratic society, because both political and economic power are in their hands. . . The unified *élite* has absolute and unbounded power.'

The major problem with the élite theories is that of stating precisely the social basis of their power, and as we have seen there is very often (in the case of Weber, Mosca and Aron, and, as critics pointed out, implicitly in the case of Mills) some kind of synthesis of class and élite conceptions. Undoubtedly, the main influence of the élite theories has been in the analysis of socialist societies, where the ruling group seemed clearly to be constituted on the basis of a monopoly of political power, but even in this case the effective possession of the means of production, along with the claim to represent the interests of the working class, played an important role. More generally, in much recent writing (Albertoni, 1987) the élite theories have been a subject of controversy mainly in relation to conceptions of democracy, and I shall examine this issue in Chapter 4. What should be noted here is that the dramatic reconstruction of socialist societies in Eastern Europe, which began in the late 1980s, in fact took the form of an assertion of democratic rights against the dictatorial power of a self-perpetuating ruling group.

In the light of the preceding analysis of diverse conceptions of stratification, class structure, and political power in the modern industrial societies, I shall maintain the following theses in this book:

(1) The class structure of capitalist societies has become more complex, and in some respects more ambiguous, in the course of the twentieth century, especially since the Second World War.
(2) At the same time there have been significant changes in the size and composition of particular classes.
(3) In the case of some classes, and notably the working class, the relation between class situation, class consciousness, and political action has become less clearly defined and less stable.
(4) The actual development of socialist societies in the twentieth century has not brought into existence a 'classless society', except in a very limited sense, but has created new social hierarchies, the analysis of which requires new theoretical approaches.
(5) Within the system of stratification in general, these approaches need to comprehend the complicated and fluctuating relationships among classes, élites, status groups, parties, social movements, political institutions, and ideologies.

These five theses provide the framework within which, in the following chapters, the class structure of capitalist and socialist societies, and the connections between class and politics, will be more systematically explored.

NOTES

1 On slavery in the ancient world and in more recent times, see Finley (1968, 1983); on caste, Srinivas *et al.* (1959) and Dumont (1970); and on the social hierarchy in feudal societies, Bloch (1961, Part VI) and Hilton (1983).
2 J. J. Rousseau (1755), cited from the Everyman edition (1952, p. 160).
3 For an early study see Dalton (1920), and among more recent studies Scott (1982) on Britain, Domhoff (1983) on the USA,

and Bottomore and Brym (1989) on the ownership of capital in the major industrial countries.

4 This was later modified by Engels, in the light of anthropological research, to refer only to written history, excluding the early communal forms of society; and he discussed in more detail the emergence of class societies in his work on the family, private property, and the state (Engels, 1884).

5 Letter to J. Weydemeyer, 1 March 1852.

6 For example, at the first congress of the Institut International de Sociologie in 1894, Marx's social theory had a prominent place in the discussions; Sorel (1895) critically examined Durkheim's sociological method in the light of Marxist theory; Durkheim (1897) reviewed Labriola's essays on the materialist conception of history; and between 1895 and 1899 Croce (1913) published several essays on historical materialism.

7 For a useful analysis and assessment of Bernstein's views, see Gay (1952).

8 Max Weber (1918), for example, in his lecture on socialism drew directly upon Bernstein's arguments.

9 See especially Hilferding (1910, Part V).

10 I shall not be concerned here with class as a universal historical phenomenon, or with class conflict as the general 'motor of history', which lie outside the scope of this book. As I noted earlier, there are many questions and controversies about the Marxist theory of class in relation to pre-capitalist societies, and Marx himself, on one occasion at least, seemed to limit the concept of class, in a precise sense, to modern society: 'The distinction between the personal and the class individual, the accidental nature of conditions of life for the individual, appears only with the emergence of class, which itself is a product of the bourgeoisie' (Marx and Engels, 1845–6, vol. I, part Ic).

11 Contrary to a popular belief, Marx did not assert that the material standard of living of the working class must decline absolutely with the development of capitalism; his principal argument was that it would decline relative to that of the bourgeoisie, either by remaining stationary while the latter rose, or by rising less rapidly. See his brief exposition in *Wage-Labour and Capital* (1848).

12 Thus Renner (1953) analysed the emergence of a 'service class' and the transformation of the working class since Marx's day (see Bottomore and Goode, 1978, pp. 113–16); and Kautsky (1927) emphasized the multiplicity of classes and the variety of conflicts and cooperation within and between them (abridged English edn, 1988, p. 372).

13 This is implied by the functionalist theory of social stratification outlined by Davis and Moore (1945), and also to some extent by the analysis of social mobility in Lipset and Bendix (1959).

14 Nevertheless, it should be noted that elsewhere he expressed
    clearly his conviction that 'the property-owning entrepreneurial
    bourgeoisie was the only group capable of providing the lead-
    ership to maintain a dynamic society' (Bahrdt, 1965, p. 126).
15 For a study of the capitalist class in seven major industrial
    countries, see Bottomore and Brym (1989), which includes com-
    prehensive data on each country and a concluding analysis of the
    international context.
16 There is a useful discussion of some of the major studies in
    Abercrombie and Urry (1983) in the context of their own analysis
    of the middle class, which aims to combine elements of Marxist
    and Weberian theory.
17 But this, it seems clear, was intended to refer to the political
    dominance of the proletariat and allied social groups (that is,
    in Marx's view, of the immense majority of the population)
    in a socialist society, and it should be seen in the context of
    Marx's strong commitment to democracy expressed in many other
    writings (Miliband, 1983, ch. 1). Certainly, Marx's conception has
    nothing in common with Stalin's reign of terror or with the general
    Bolshevik doctrine of the monopolization of political power by a
    single party.
18 For a useful critical summary of the different approaches, see
    Abercrombie and Urry (1983, chs 2 and 3).
19 These Weberian distinctions have some importance in analysing
    the political orientations of particular social groups in capitalist
    societies (and to some extent in socialist societies), and will be
    considered more fully in a later chapter.

2

Classes in Modern Capitalism

Britain in the mid-nineteenth century was taken by Marx as his model of the development of capitalism and the formation of the 'two great classes' in modern society, although he associated with this a model of class conflict and revolution derived mainly from the experience of France[1] and from the revolutions of 1848 in Europe. Many other social observers noted the growing rift in British society, among them Disraeli, who gave a vivid description in his novel *Sybil* (1845) of the emergence of 'two nations', and at the same time set out to turn this to political advantage by enlisting the support of industrial workers for the Tory party against the Whigs. But the class system in Britain also had some peculiar features which arose, in the words of Tawney (1952), from 'the blend of a crude plutocratic reality with the sentimental aroma of an aristocratic legend'. Out of this situation grew the 'gentleman ideal',[2] the public schools as agencies for consolidating and transmitting it, and what Matthew Arnold called the 'religion of inequality', which pervaded, and still pervades, British social life to a remarkable degree.

Later writers have documented more fully this feature of the British class structure, and its connection with the development of British capitalism. Wiener (1981) argues that, while at the time of the Great Exhibition of 1851 Britain 'was the home of the industrial revolution, a symbol of material progress . . . the home of an apparently triumphant bourgeoisie' (p. 157), this picture was misleading as an indicator of future development, for the persistence and wide diffusion of aristocratic and gentry values have steadily undermined the 'industrial spirit' up to the present day. Rubinstein (1987) has documented the dominant position in the class structure, up to the First

World War, of landowners, merchants and financiers, as against industrialists, and the subsequent emergence of a more unified élite or class, which is, however, dominated by 'the south of England and finance' (p. 70), not by industrial capital. Much earlier, Hilferding (1910, chs 21 and 22) had noted that British capitalism was being overtaken by the more advanced economies of the United States and Germany; and the economic decline of Britain has continued inexorably throughout this century, so that today Japan, the United States, and most member countries of the European Community, as well as Sweden and Austria, are far ahead in their economic development.

The class structure of every capitalist society has, of course, some individual distinguishing features, arising from events in its historical development and from particular cultural characteristics, but the society which, besides Britain, displays the most distinctive features is the United States. It was in the general acceptance of an egalitarian ideology, which still persists in some degree, that this society differed most remarkably from the European countries in the nineteenth century. In the United States, there was no established system of feudal ranks, no historical memory of an aristocratic order of society, which could provide a model for a new social hierarchy. The American war of independence indeed was an important influence upon the European revolutions against the *ancien régime*. Here, in contrast with the European countries, the ownership of property was quite widely diffused in the early part of the nineteenth century, and some 80 per cent of the working population (excluding the Negro slaves) owned the means of production with which they worked. America was, predominantly, a society of small farmers, small traders and small businessmen – the closest approach there has ever been to a 'property-owning democracy'. Of course, disparities of wealth existed, but they were not so extreme as in Europe, and they did not give rise, except in some of the southern states, to differences of social rank comparable with those in the still aristocratic and oligarchical European societies. Tocqueville (1835) saw in the United States the prime example of a tendency towards equality in modern societies; a society in which, as he wrote: 'Great wealth tends to disappear, the number of small fortunes to increase.'

The sense of belonging to a society of equals was enhanced by the possibility of easy movement in the still rudimentary hierarchy of wealth. America was the 'land of opportunity', a vast, unexplored and unexploited country in which it was always possible, or seemed possible, to escape from economic want or subjection by moving to a new place, acquiring land or some other property, and adding to it by personal effort and talent.

A century and a half of economic change has destroyed most of the foundations upon which the egalitarian ideology rested. The society made up of small property-owners and independent producers began to be undermined soon after the Civil War, and the 1880s and 1890s, a period in which industry grew rapidly and modern communications were vastly expanded, saw the 'closing of the frontier', the emergence of the first industrial and financial trusts, and a considerable growth of inequalities of wealth. Class divisions began to appear more clearly, to resemble more closely those in the European societies, and to be more openly asserted.[3] The conscious emergence of an upper class was signalled by the establishment of the *Social Register* (the guide to the new American 'aristocracy'), and by the foundation of exclusive boarding schools and country clubs; and wealth and social position came increasingly to be transmitted through family connections. At the same time, the working class became more strongly organized in trade unions and political associations, and from the 1890s to the 1930s there were numerous attempts, though without any lasting success, to bring these associations together in a broad socialist movement.

Early in the nineteenth century, 80 per cent of the active white population were independent (self-employed) producers; by 1870 only 41 per cent were self-employed, and by 1940 only 18 per cent. In the words of C. Wright Mills (1951, p. 34): 'Over the last hundred years, the United States has been transformed from a nation of small capitalists into a nation of hired employees; but the ideology suitable for the nation of small capitalists persists, as if that small-propertied world were still a going concern.'

There are several reasons for the persistence of this inept ideology, apart from the inertia which characterizes social doctrines in general. One is that the concentration of property ownership was not accompanied by any sudden expansion of the working class, or by any decline in the standard of living. Industrial workers formed 28 per cent of the population in 1870, and 31 per cent in 1940; and wage-earners as a whole made up 53 per cent of the population in 1870, and 57 per cent in 1940. During the same period, however, the proportion of salaried employees in the population increased very rapidly, from 7 per cent to 25 per cent; and this expansion of the new white-collar middle class made possible a new kind of social mobility, in place of that which had been achieved earlier by the settlement of fresh lands. The massive immigration from continental Europe in the first two decades of this century, the continued growth of the economy during most of this period, and other factors which will be referred to later in discussing the general characteristics of the class structure have all contributed to the persistence of this egalitarian doctrine.

The particular features of class relations in individual countries – most marked, as I have suggested, in Britain and the United States, but also apparent in a more general contrast between Europe and the United States or Japan – do not, however, obliterate the fundamental characteristics of the class structure in capitalist societies and the changes it has undergone in the past hundred years. By the end of the nineteenth century, in all the developed capitalist countries, there was a massive accumulation of wealth in the hands of the 'upper ten thousand',[4] and severe poverty at the other end of the social hierarchy. The situation in Britain will illustrate a general phenomenon. Charles Booth's (1891–1903) survey of London, carried out between 1887 and 1891, showed 30 per cent of the inhabitants living in poverty, and similar conclusions emerged from Rowntree's (1901) study of social conditions in York, begun in 1899. In the same period, and up to the First World War, a privileged 1 per cent of the population owned 68 per cent of all private property and received 29 per cent of the total national income.

But this situation was already beginning to change, as was demonstrated in the debate provoked by Bernstein's book (see page 12 above), in which the growth of the middle class, a wider diffusion of property ownership, and generally rising standards of living were seen as modifying class relations. To these factors may be added the influence of the rapid growth of socialist parties, especially in continental Europe, which had as one of its consequences a gradual increase in government expenditure on social welfare, financed by new taxes. In Britain, following the introduction of income tax, an estate duty was imposed towards the end of the nineteenth century, though initially at a very low rate which reduced large fortunes very slowly, if at all; and the effects of higher rates introduced during the present century were counteracted by various forms of tax avoidance and by capital gains in periods of expansion.

Nevertheless, there have been important changes during the present century, and in particular since 1945. In Britain, the changes in the distribution of wealth and income were very modest up to 1939. Thus the top 1 per cent of the population owned 61 per cent of all private wealth in 1923 and 55 per cent in 1938 (the top 10 per cent owned 89 per cent in 1923 and 85 per cent in 1938), while the bottom 80 per cent of the population owned only 6 per cent in 1923 and 9 per cent in 1938 (Pond, 1983, p. 11, figures rounded). Studies of income distribution suggest that over the period 1900–39 there was little redistribution in favour of wage-earners: at the end of the period, 10 per cent of the population received almost half the total national income while 90 per cent shared the other half. This distribution is what might be expected from the fact that a substantial part of the income of the upper class comes from earnings on property, and that the economic depression of the 1930s with its mass unemployment significantly reduced the incomes of wage-earners, a situation only slightly mitigated by a modest increase in government expenditure on social welfare.

From 1945 until the 1970s there was a continuing redistribution of wealth and income in Britain, although at a slower pace than has sometimes been supposed. Pond (1983, p. 11) estimated that by 1972 the top 1 per cent of the population still owned 32 per cent of wealth (the top 10 per cent owned some 70 per cent), while the bottom 80 per cent had no more than 15 per cent. The distribution of income has also changed rather slowly, though it differs significantly from the pre-war period: after tax, the top 10 per cent of the population received 27 per cent of national income in 1949 and 23 per cent in 1978/9, while the bottom 50 per cent of the population received 26 per cent in 1949 and the same proportion in 1978/9 (Playford and Pond, 1983, p. 39). Since 1979, the inequalities of wealth and income have tended to increase again, as a result of tax changes and the contraction of public expenditure on social welfare.

Although Britain may have 'the doubtful distinction of leading the international inequality league' (Atkinson, 1974, p. 21),[5] the situation in all the major capitalist countries is broadly similar; it is clear that over the post-war period as a whole the capitalist class has largely succeeded in maintaining its economic and political dominance (Bottomore and Brym, 1989), even though in some countries it may appear difficult to define.[6] In a few countries, however, and notably in those (such as Sweden and Austria) which I have described elsewhere as 'socialistic' (Bottomore, 1990), an extension of public ownership, a degree of central planning, and highly developed welfare systems, brought about by strong socialist parties, have restricted the power of the capitalist class and created a more egalitarian society.

The general dominance of the capitalist class, which has been strangely ignored, or underestimated, in much of the post-war writing on class and stratification, can be explained in part by the initial advantages which this class enjoys as an 'organized minority' possessing substantial resources, both economic and cultural, to enable it to represent itself as a 'natural' and effective ruling group. But it has also to be explained, to a large extent, by the changes in other classes in the context of post-war economic development, and by the historical evolution of socialist societies over the same period.

Let us consider first the general economic conditions. In Western Europe, North America, and Japan, economic growth after 1945 was exceptionally rapid, and more stable than in earlier periods.[7] This economic upsurge was associated with an extension of economic planning and government regulation of the economy in most countries, and with a substantial increase in public expenditure, which accounted, by the 1970s, for between 40 and 50 per cent of GDP. From this transformation there emerged the 'welfare capitalism' and the 'mixed economies' of the 1960s, which had important consequences for the class structure and class relations.

Both Rowntree and Booth concluded from their investigations that two of the most important causes of poverty were the lack of regular employment and the expenses of protracted ill-health. The improvement in conditions of life for the working class in the post-war capitalist societies obviously owed much to the maintenance of full employment, and to the development of national health services (though this has been less adequate in the United States). Full employment, besides raising the level of income of the working class and providing a degree of that economic security which the upper class has always taken for granted, has almost entirely eliminated the class of domestic servants; this escape from one particularly onerous form of subjection to another class[8] is one of the greatest gains which the European working class has made in the twentieth century.

It may be argued, too, that the social services as a whole have a much greater effect in diminishing class differences than would appear from their economic consequences alone. As Tawney (1952, p. 248) wrote:

> There are certain gross and crushing disabilities – conditions of life injurious to health, inferior education, economic insecurity . . . which place the classes experiencing them at a permanent disadvantage with those not similarly afflicted. There are certain services by which these crucial disabilities have been greatly mitigated, and, given time and will, can be altogether removed. . . . The contribution to equality made by these dynamic agencies is obviously out of all proportion greater than that which would result from an annual present to every individual among the forty odd millions concerned of a sum equivalent to his quota of the total cost.

The social services not only help to create an equality in the vital conditions of life for all citizens; so far as they are used by everyone, the standard of the service tends to rise. It may well be true, as some have argued, that the middle class has benefited at least as much as the working class from the expansion of the social services, but one important consequence has been that, for example, the standards of free medical care have been vastly improved as compared with the time when such care was provided only for the poor and needy. In the field of education, similar progress was evident in Britain as a result of the Education Act of 1944, although here class differences have proved more tenacious and difficult to overcome, while the existence of a large (and now growing) private sector of education used by the wealthier groups in society has meant that there has been less vigour in the drive to improve the standard of the public service, especially in comparison with other European countries.

We may conclude that the general advance in the material conditions of the working class in Britain and other capitalist societies during the past forty years has been due largely to the rapid growth of national income, which has also made possible the expansion of the social services, rather than to any radical redistribution of wealth or income between classes. Moreover, even in these more affluent societies a great deal of poverty remains. Its significance for the relations between classes is, however, very different from that which it had in the nineteenth century and the first decades of the twentieth century. Then poverty was the lot of a whole class, and there was no expectation that it could be quickly alleviated within the limits of the capitalist economic system. It separated one class in society distinctly from others, and at the same time engendered a movement of revolt. In the present-day advanced capitalist countries, poverty has largely ceased to be of this kind. It is now less extensive, and is confined to particular groups in the population – old people dependent on state pensions, workers in certain occupations or regions which have been left behind as a result of technological progress, and other groups of low-paid workers, some ethnic groups (notably in the United States), immigrant workers in some countries, and the unemployed – which, although they constitute a significant proportion of the population (as high as 25 per cent in some cases), are generally too isolated, unorganized, or heterogeneous to provide the basis of a radical social movement. These impoverished groups stand in marked contrast with a majority of the working class, which now has a relatively high standard of living compared with its situation half a century ago.

The thesis of embourgeoisement, which was briefly examined earlier, relies in the main for its factual basis upon this improvement in living standards and the changes in the relative economic position of manual workers and some sections of white-collar workers, but it also brings in the effects of social mobility in modifying the class system. Since the war, sociologists have studied social mobility as much as they have studied the changes within classes themselves, and many of them have attributed great importance to it as a solvent of class divisions. The findings of some of the major studies[9] may be summarized in the following way. Social mobility has generally increased with the economic development of all modern industrial societies, but the increase has been due largely to changes in the occupational structure; that is, to the expansion of white-collar and professional occupations and the contraction of manual occupations. There is relatively little exchange of personnel between classes, and Miller (1960, p. 59) suggested that sociologists should give more attention to the extent of 'downward mobility', which involves a real exchange of occupational and social position, and may well be 'a better indicator of fluidity in a society than is upward mobility'.

A second important feature is that most social mobility takes place between social levels which are close together; for example, between the upper strata of the working class and the lower strata of the middle class. Movement from the working class into the upper class is very limited in any capitalist society, as is shown by the reproduction of a capitalist class through the transmission of family wealth (Bottomore and Brym, 1989), by estimates of the life-chances of individuals from different classes in respect of attaining a position in the economic and social élite (Heath, 1981, p. 77), and by studies of recruitment to particular élite occupations. Thus, a study of the directors of large companies in Britain (Copeman, 1955) showed that more than half of them began their careers with the advantage of having business connections in the family, while another 40 per cent came from families of landowners, professional people and others of similar social position. Similarly, a study of top civil servants showed that 30 per cent came from families of the upper and upper middle class, another 40 per cent from intermediate levels of the middle class, and only 3 per cent from families of semi-skilled and unskilled workers, although there were indications that the social area of recruitment had been broadened somewhat since the 1930s (Kelsall, 1955). My own research on the higher civil service in France showed that, even after the post-war reforms, 65 per cent of those accepted for entry to the top ranks of the civil service via the *École Nationale d'Administration* came from families of the upper and upper middle class, 28 per cent from intermediate levels of the middle class, and 7 per cent from families of farmers and skilled workers (Bottomore, 1952).

It was sometimes supposed that the relative 'classlessness' (in a social and cultural sense) of American society could be explained in part by a higher rate of social mobility than in European countries. But although this may have been true for the first half of the nineteenth century (when geographical mobility, in a continent still incompletely explored and settled, was an important component, and the egalitarian ideology was reinforced by wide diffusion of small property ownership), international comparisons suggest that more recently the United States has not had an exceptionally high rate of social mobility (Lipset and Bendix, 1959; Heath, 1981, ch. 7), in terms either of movement from manual to non-manual occupations, or of recruitment to the élite. Heath (1981), in particular, examines the difficulties inherent in making international comparisons, and the variable results which may be produced by alternative methods of analysis. He concludes that, while there is a relatively high rate of mobility into the élite and across the manual/non-manual line in all modern industrial societies, connected with changes in the occupational structure, there are significant but not massive differences among capitalist countries (with 'new' and more socialistic countries having the highest rates, more conservative countries and those which had periods of fascist rule the lowest), while in the socialist countries of Eastern Europe there have been particularly high rates of inflow into élite and white-collar occupations (which I shall discuss in the next chapter).

The actual degree of social mobility, even if its range is limited, and the sense of living in a more 'open' and fluid society, have affected the working class in two ways. First, as Hilferding (1910) already noted with reference to those who had entered the lower levels of white-collar employment, the possibility of advancement in the social hierarchy kindles individual ambition and weakens the feeling of class solidarity (see page 15 above), and this raises questions about class consciousness which will be considered in Chapter 4. Second, the changes in the occupational structure brought about by the development of capitalist production in the era of 'organized' and 'welfare' capitalism, and the consequent large-scale movement into clerical, technical, and professional employment (both public and private), have steadily reduced the size of the working class while increasing the numbers of the middle class. The changes in Britain, which are fairly typical of the general process,[10] have been studied by Routh (1980), who shows that between 1911 and 1971 (and most rapidly since 1945) the proportion of professional people, employers and managers in the occupied population rose from 14 per cent to 23.5 per cent, and of clerical workers from 5 per cent to 14 per cent, while the proportion of the group comprising foremen and manual workers fell from 81 per cent to 63 per cent (p. 5, figures rounded), and had fallen again to 54 per cent by 1979 (p. 45). Today, in all the advanced capitalist countries the working class comprises less than 50 per cent of the population. This is a situation very different from that envisaged by Marx, and by many later Marxists up to the 1930s, in which the working class as 'the immense majority' of the population would accomplish a social revolution.

The growth of the middle class, although it was recognized by Marxists and other social scientists from the end of the nineteenth century (and even, *en passant*, by Marx; see above page 11), has become a major preoccupation of students of the class system only since the 1950s, and its composition, social location, and political affiliations are the subject of diverse interpretation and much controversy. The first thing to be said is that the middle class is extremely heterogeneous and differentiated, so that many social scientists have been inclined to speak of the 'middle classes' in the plural, and in effect to define the various categories which compose it as 'status groups' even though these may sometimes, confusingly, be referred to as 'classes' (e.g. the lower middle class). This tendency to rely exclusively upon one element in Weber's analytical scheme (which encompassed class, status and power) is apparent in Mills's (1951) study of American white-collar workers, and it may lead, as it does to some extent in his work, to a conception of the whole stratification system as a hierarchy of status groups, in which a highly differentiated middle class merges at one end of the scale into various élite groups and at the other end into the upper levels of the category of manual workers (the skilled or 'affluent' workers).[11]

Other social scientists, while making use of the Weberian concept of status in various ways, have been primarily concerned with demarcating the boundaries which separate the middle class from the working class and from the capitalist class (or 'upper class'). The studies of the 'boundary problem' have produced very diverse accounts of the class structure, and in particular major disagreements between those who are more Weberian or more Marxist in their approach.[12] One notable study by Lockwood (1958) used a comprehensive Weberian approach to define the differences between clerical workers and manual workers in terms of three factors – work situation, market situation, and status position – and concluded that 'as soon as the term "class situation" is understood to cover not only market situation but also work situation, it is clear that clerk and manual worker do not, in most cases, share the same class situation at all' (p. 280). Giddens (1973) in the main adopted a similar approach, emphasizing market situation and reaching a similar conclusion about the class differences between manual and white-collar workers, but expounded a more Marxist–Weberian conception of the class system as a whole, in which possession or non-possession of property are the basic categories of class position.

Marxist accounts of the boundary between the middle class and the working class have followed two main directions.[13] One group of theorists takes as a central theme the 'proletarianization' of the middle class, or major sections of it. This thesis, already propounded by several writers in the 1930s in the context of the economic depression (e.g. Corey, 1935; Klingender, 1935), was later developed by Renner (1953), who argued, in the course of his analysis of the 'service class' as a new type of middle class, that 'the majority of its members have become in practice propertyless', and thus 'the service class is closer to the rising working class in its life style, and at its boundary tends to merge with it'. Another aspect of the proletarianization of the middle class was emphasized by Braverman (1974) in his argument concerning the 'deskilling' of clerical labour as a result of changes in capitalist production, which were not, however, very fully explored.

The studies of proletarianization concentrated for the most part on economic changes and tended to ignore the question of whether such changes were accompanied, or likely to be accompanied, by the emergence of new social and political attitudes in the middle class. Among the second group of Marxist thinkers, who rejected the 'proletarianization' thesis, and especially in the work of Poulantzas (1968, 1974), ideological and political factors are given equal importance with economic relations in the constitution of a social class. Poulantzas' main thesis is that the middle class (petty bourgeoisie), which includes both the traditional and the new middle class, is a distinctive class, sharply separated from the working class. However, this, along with his very restrictive definition of the working class, poses many problems for his analysis of the political implications of the changging class structure, which will be considered in Chapter 4. Others who reject the proletarianization thesis recognize the distinctiveness of middle-class groups in various ways, concentrating in some cases on the situation of professional and managerial personnel, or arguing (Wright, 1978) that between the capitalist class and the working class there are intermediate strata whose members occupy 'contradictory class locations'.

These studies lead on to the question of the relationship between the upper levels of the middle class and the capitalist class, and the extent to which they are merging in a new type of dominant class. Abercrombie and Urry (1983, ch. 8 and Conclusion) argue that the causal powerrs of both capital and

labour have been weakened as a result of the later development of capitalism, while the causal powers of the 'service
class' (which they define in a different way from Renner,
distinguishing it from the category of deskilled white-collar
workers) have increased, and this class is 'taking on, and
concentrating within itself, the functions of capital, namely,
conceptualisation, control, and reproduction', while the 'class
position of the capitalist class is being transformed, and its
functions are becoming somewhat indistinguishable from those
of the service class . . . The process of class formation . . . is
increasingly the outcome of the distribution of hierarchically
ordered educational credentials' (p. 153). This thesis is similar
to that which Touraine (1971) expounded in his analysis of the
new 'post-industrial society', in which property has ceased to
be the criterion of membership in the dominant class, and 'the
new dominant class is defined by knowledge and a certain level
of education'. But this argument can be disputed, and has been
disputed, on the basis of studies of the present-day capitalist
class (Scott, 1982; Bottomore and Brym, 1989), which show the
immense power of family wealth in establishing control over the
large corporations that dominate economic life.

The political consequences of this economic domination will
be elaborated in Chapter 4, but some preliminary observations
can be made at this point. The 'service class', as a part of
the middle class, does not displace the capitalist class in the
domination of society, nor does it merge with the capitalist class
to any considerable extent. It does play an important part in the
management and regulation of many vital economic and social
agencies (public and private corporations, the administration
of welfare), but primarily in a subaltern role as the executor
of decisions made elsewhere. The growth of the middle class
as a whole is, however, important in two other ways. First, it
increases the diversity of civil society and gives rise to new
forms of political activity, which tend to reduce the influence
of class-based politics, though mainly at the expense of the
working class, whereas the class struggle from above by the
capitalist class is much less affected. This is also partly because,
secondly, a large part of the middle class tends generally,
by virtue of its economic and social situation, to support a

capitalist economic order. As Marx commented in one of his brief references to the subject, the continually growing middle classes 'rest with all their weight upon the working class and at the same time increase the social security and power of the upper ten thousand' (see above, page 11). Similarly, though in the framework of his élite theory, Mosca observed that the 'political class' or governing élite is intimately connected with society through a sub-élite (comprising virtually the whole 'new middle class'), which is a vital element in the government of society, so that 'the stability of any political organism depends on the level of morality, intelligence and activity that this second stratum has attained' (Bottomore, 1964, p. 11).

The nature of the class system in advanced capitalist societies is manifestly a highly contentious issue, further aspects of which I shall explore later. For the present, I shall summarize my own conception of it based upon the preceding analysis of divergent interpretations. This class system, which is in a process of continual change, has the following principal characteristics:

(1) There is a dominant capitalist class, sustained by family wealth and corporate power, which is in some respects more powerful than it has ever been as a result of the growth of large, and frequently multinational, corporations, which dominate the economy. In other respects, however, its dominance has been circumscribed (to varying degrees in different countries) by the growth of state intervention in the economy, a limited extension of public ownership, and greatly increased public expenditure, all of which withdraw substantial resources from the sphere of capitalist profit-making and the accumulation process, and have been achieved largely by the continuous efforts of working-class parties to modify or transform capitalist society.

(2) The middle class has continually increased in numbers, and its social and political importance has grown in consequence. It is, however, the most heterogeneous of the social classes – differentiated in terms of self-employment or employment by others, employment in public or private enterprises and agencies, and levels of income, property

ownership and education – and characterized by diverse and fluctuating social and political orientations, although the predominant tendency is normally to acquiesce in or support a capitalist market economy (qualified in some cases by ideas of 'welfare capitalism', a 'mixed economy', or a 'social market economy').

(3) The working class has diminished as a proportion of the population, and more recently in absolute numbers, so that some former Marxists, and other socialists, have bade 'farewell to the working class' (Gorz, 1982). However, this interpretation needs to be examined in the context of arguments about the emergence of a 'new working class', and of the growing political influence of socialist and labour parties in most of Western Europe since 1945, while taking account of the changing conceptions of 'socialism' itself.

During the twentieth century the socialist alternative to capitalism, like the capitalist class system, has passed through a complex process of change, in which a major element has been the historical course taken by socialist societies as they were established, and evolved, first in Russia and after 1945 in other countries of Eastern Europe, in China, and elsewhere. The next chapter, therefore, will be devoted to an analysis of class and classlessness in these societies, a subject which has generated wide-ranging controversies that illuminate many aspects of the processes of class formation and of social stratification in general. These questions gain a new significance in the conditions which have emerged from the tumultuous changes in Eastern Europe in the late 1980s.

NOTES

1 Marx's conception of the working class and its political role was influenced in some degree by Lorenz von Stein's book (1842, enlarged edn 1850) on the socialist movement in France (see Avineri, 1968, pp. 52–64), but he also emphasized the importance of the Chartists in Britain (Marx, 1852).

2 The question of who is a 'gentleman', how he is formed, and what social values he expresses, is a major theme in the novels

of Thackeray and (especially) Trollope (see Gilmour, 1981). The same theme was taken up from a different point of view by Alfred Marshall, in a paper on 'The future of the working classes' (1873), who argued that as a result of the growth of education and leisure a condition of society would be reached in which, 'by occupation at least, every man is a gentleman'; and this idea in turn formed the starting point for T. H. Marshall's (1950) study of citizenship and social class.

3 In the words of Beard (1914), describing the American scene at the end of the nineteenth century, the men of affairs and political leaders 'believed in the widest possible extension of the principle of private property, and the narrowest possible restriction of state interference, except to aid private property to increase its gains' (p. 53). As a result, 'Deep underlying class feeling found its expression in the conventions of both parties, and particularly that of the Democrats, and forced upon the attention of the country, in a dramatic manner, a conflict between great wealth and the lower middle and working classes, which had hitherto been recognized only in obscure circles' (p. 164).

4 An expression used by Trollope in the first sentence of *Can You Forgive Her?* (1864) and elsewhere, and also by Marx in the manuscript of *Theories of Surplus Value* (1861–3). It seems to have been taken from an American writer, and to have been in current use in the 1860s (Stephen Wall, 1972, in the Penguin edition of *Can You Forgive Her?*). A similar, though more restrictive term, the 'two hundred families', was widely used in France at a later time.

5 In this highly inegalitarian class system the aristocracy still has a prominent place, as Sampson (1962, pp. 4–5) remarked:

> the aristocracy are, in general, much richer than they seem. With democracy has come discretion. Their London palaces and outward show have disappeared, but the countryside is still full of millionaire peers: many of them with the boom in property, are richer now than they have ever been.

Scott (1982, p. 134) estimated that in 1967 'about 200 peerage families holding estates of 5,000 acres or more owned about one-third of the British land area'.

6 See Spohn and Bodemann (1989, pp. 73–4), who suggest some reasons for this in the Federal Republic of Germany:

> First, there is no stratum of capitalists . . . that is a self-conscious, socially cohesive ruling group . . . Second, there is little similarity between the sharp class antagonisms of Imperial Germany and the relatively stable contemporary . . .

> social structure . . . Third, workers and employers no longer think that they live in a class-divided society . . . the idea of a 'social partnership' between employers and employees prevails and there has emerged a general consensus based on political democracy and the welfare state.

Nevertheless, they conclude 'that over the past two decades, the West German capitalist class has been increasingly consolidated' (p. 100).

7 Postan (1967) calculated that between 1918 and 1938 productivity in Western Europe increased by 1.7 per cent per annum, whereas between 1945 and 1963 it increased at 3.5 per cent per annum, and the aggregate GNP was two and a half times greater in 1963 than in 1938. At the same time, this post-war boom suffered far less from recurrent crises of the pre-war kind. See also Maddison (1982, p. 96), who shows that productivity performance in sixteen capitalist countries accelerated greatly in what he calls the 'Golden Age', from 1950 to 1973.

8 Marx observed in *Capital*, vol. I, that the vast increase in the numbers of domestic servants, of whom there were well over 1 million in Britain in 1861, showed clearly the growing divergence between the classes, with wealth and luxury concentrated at one extreme, poverty and servitude at the other.

9 The first comprehensive national study in Britain, by Glass *et al.* (1954), provided a model for several later investigations, and it was replicated (with various modifications) twenty-five years later in the Oxford mobility enquiry (Goldthorpe, 1980). Some international comparisons have also been undertaken, by Lipset and Bendix (1959), Miller (1960), and more recently Heath (1981, ch. 7).

10 Although there are some significant differences between countries, briefly discussed by Routh (1980, pp. 9–12).

11 See the discussion in Abercrombie and Urry (1983, pp. 15–17), who also go on to consider other approaches inspired by more or less Weberian conceptions.

12 See Abercrombie and Urry (1983, chs 2–5) for a general comment.

13 See the discussion and references in Abercrombie and Urry (1983, chs 4–5).

3
Class, Classlessness and Socialism

According to Marx's view, modern capitalism would be 'the last antagonistic form of the process of production', and, as he wrote in *The Poverty of Philosophy* (1847):

> The condition for the emancipation of the working class is the abolition of all classes . . . . The working class, in the course of its development, will substitute for the old civil society an association which will exclude classes and their antagonism.

The USSR, although the revolution which created it did not take place in a highly industrialized capitalist country, has nevertheless claimed to be a society of the kind which Marx predicted would follow the destruction of capitalism; that is to say, a classless society, at least in the sense that there is no hierarchy of classes and no domination by one class over others. This claim was based mainly upon the fact that the private ownership of the means of production had been abolished. Social scientists in the USSR have rarely attempted to analyse the social and political foundations of a classless society, and for long periods, especially after 1930, they were at some pains to make a sharp distinction between 'classlessness' and 'egalitarianism'. The latter was denounced as a 'petty bourgeois deviation', and the Soviet Encyclopaedia of Stalin's time asserted that 'socialism and egalitarianism have nothing in common.'[1]

This ideological offensive against egalitarianism coincided broadly with the change in policy of the Soviet rulers in the early 1930s, which involved increasing wage and salary differentials, and in particular offering substantial financial incentives to highly skilled workers, scientists and technicians, industrial managers and intellectuals. These policies were continued during and after the war, and as a result the range of earned incomes in the USSR came to be almost as great as that in the capitalist countries. It is estimated that in 1953 industrial incomes ranged between 3,500 and 5,000 roubles a year for an unskilled worker, and between 80,000 and 120,000 roubles for an important factory manager. The top incomes were, therefore, some twenty-five to thirty times as great as those at the bottom. This was perhaps somewhat less than the difference in most capitalist countries at that time between the income of an unskilled worker and that of a managing director, but when the effects of taxation are taken into account the income range in the USSR may have been rather greater, because the Soviet income tax was not steeply progressive, and taxation as a whole was regressive, since the greater part of the budget income was derived from a turnover tax on food and textile goods of mass consumption. These inequalities of income were enhanced by other factors: by the abolition of the progressive inheritance tax in 1943, and by the privileges accorded to the higher social strata in education and housing, the use of special shops, the acquisition of cars and other scarce goods, and the award of prizes, grants and annuities.

The policy of increasing income differentiation could be explained to some extent by the demands of rapid industrialization in the 1930s, and later by the needs of war and post-war reconstruction. This is not, I think, the whole explanation; but in so far as it contains some truth, we might expect that with the completion of basic industrialization and reconstruction there would be a slackening, or even a reversal, of the trend towards greater inequality. A later study (Yanowitch, 1963) suggested that this was in fact happening. The author observed that after 1956 a number of policy statements emphasized the raising of minimum wages and quoted the programme of the 22nd Congress of the CPSU to the effect that in the next twenty years 'the disparity between high and comparatively low incomes must be steadily reduced'. He went on to calculate from Soviet statistics (which became somewhat more abundant and accessible) that wage differentials declined considerably after 1956; for example, whereas the average earnings of engineering technical personnel exceeded those of manual workers by two and a half times in the early 1930s, they were only 50 per cent higher in 1960. He concluded: 'The period since 1956 has been marked by a narrowing of skill differentials in wage rates, substantial increases in minimum wages, and the declining importance of the piece-rate system.'

In the other socialist countries of Eastern Europe, income differentials were probably similar and followed a similar course of development, if not quite so markedly anti-egalitarian at any stage, although the absence of comprehensive and systematic studies has always made it difficult, if not impossible, to present a detailed and definitive picture. One major difference between socialist and capitalist societies should, however, be emphasized at this point. In the former, income distribution refers only to *earned* income, and there has not been, for any section of the population, the possibility of a significant *unearned* income from the accumulation and inheritance of wealth, which plays such an important part in the affluence of the upper class in capitalist society.

This is one of the considerations which has sustained the view that economic inequalities in the Soviet Union, and subsequently in other socialist societies, did not signify the growth of a new class system. One sympathetic French observer of Soviet society (Gordey, 1952) put the argument as follows:

> Some people might be tempted to conclude on the basis of this profound wage differentiation that Soviet society has not, in reality, abolished classes. . . . It seems to me that classes as they exist in Western countries have actually no true equivalent in the USSR. The prejudices based on wealth, rigid barriers, the organized opposition of one class to its enlargement from below – these no longer exist or are in process of disappearing for ever in the Soviet Union. Widespread education, the encouragement profusely given by the authorities to the social advance of those elements which have been less well placed to start with – all this points towards a final result that may legitimately be termed

a 'classless society.' . . . That is why, if anyone may argue about the presence or absence of classes in the USSR, one must in any case recognize that the upper classes are abundantly open to members of the lower classes, and that the privileged levels have nothing of crystallization, rigidity, or especially heredity about them.

A number of sociologists have also taken the view that social classes, in any form resembling that which they have in capitalist societies, do not exist in the socialist countries. Parkin (1971, ch. 5) argued that the reward structure of socialist societies could not be represented 'as a dichotomous class model on the Western pattern, since there is a much less obvious "break" between manual and non-manual positions' (p. 147). At the same time, there are more opportunities for upward mobility within the manual class (p. 148). On the other hand, there is a distinct boundary between the white-collar intelligentsia and other groups in the occupational structure. The intelligentsia, closely allied with the Communist Party and enjoying all kinds of economic and social privileges, might be regarded as forming a new dominant class. However, this still differs significantly from the upper class in capitalist societies in not being a closed and socially exclusive group. In consequence, there is less normative differentiation along class lines, and little evidence of a 'working-class subculture' such as exists under capitalism. Parkin concluded that:

> if we take a synchronic view of the present socialist reward system we can detect a distinct social boundary between the 'new class' and the rest of society. We should thus be justified in regarding it as a class system in this restricted sense. If, on the other hand, we take a diachronic view of the same system we are bound to note that this boundary is a highly permeable one in the sense that movement into the 'new class' from below is continuously taking place. Seen from this angle, the 'classlessness' thesis has greater plausibility. (1971, p. 158)

A similar view was expounded by Weselowski (1979) in his study of Polish society, in which he disputed the idea that a new dominant class was being formed, while recognizing that status differences persisted, as well as conflicts of interest between different social groups and strata.

Against such conceptions other social scientists have argued that a new class system, or a distinctive hierarchical order, was created in the Soviet Union and subsequently in other socialist countries. Djilas (1957) employed a distinction between 'juridical ownership' and 'effective possession' of property, later elaborated by Hegedüs (1976, ch. 7), to argue that there had emerged in the Soviet Union a distinct social group of 'owners of the means of production' in the latter sense, comprising the leading officials of the Communist Party and the apparatus of economic planning and management, which constituted a new exploitative class resembling the former bourgeoisie, in a type of society that might be described as 'state capitalism'. Similarly, in the light of Hungarian experience, Konrád and Szelényi (1979, p. 145) argued that:

> the social structure of early socialism is organized in keeping with the principle of rational redistribution. In line with the rational principle on which its economy is based, we regard this as a class structure, and indeed a dichotomous one. At one pole is an evolving class of intellectuals who occupy the position of redistributors, at the other a working class which produces the social surplus but has no right of disposition over it.

However, they also noted that not everyone in the society could be assigned to one or other of these groups, and that just as in capitalist society 'an ever larger fraction of the population must be assigned to the intermediate strata'. In a later chapter (ch. 12) they considered the conflict of interest between the redistributors and the working class, which does not appear in the form of clearly formulated class interests, because it cannot be articulated openly, but is evident at the level of everyday consciousness.

The question remains, however, whether these clearly distinguishable groups in the socialist countries – in particular, redistributors or bureaucrats on one side, industrial workers on the other – can properly be defined as classes in the framework of Marxist or other theories. Many social scientists have rejected such definitions, while at the same time denying that these societies are 'classless' in the wider sense of being egalitarian and non-exploitative. For them, the crucial feature is the domination exercised by a one-party state over the rest of the population; as Ossowski argued (see above, page 24–5), where political authorities can effectively change the class structure we are a long way from the interpretations of class by Marx and others who conceived classes as groups determined by their relation to the means of production. The difference may be summarized by saying that the bureaucracy, or 'redistributors', or '*nomenklatura*', are the 'effective possessors' of the means of production *because* they have political power; they are *not* a dominant or ruling class as a consequence of being, in the first place, the 'owners' of the means of production.

What has been increasingly emphasized, therefore, in the structure of socialist societies, is the concentration of political power in a single party which excludes any opposition and rules by totalitarian means.[2] Thus Hilferding (1940, 1941) defined the Soviet Union as a 'totalitarian state economy', and went on to reassess the Marxist conception of history in the light of the growth of state power which accompanies the development of the modern economy, and the gradual 'subordination of all historically significant social processes to the conscious will of the state'. Other social scientists, and notably Raymond Aron, took elements from the élite theories (see above, page 17) in order to establish a contrast between the plurality of élites in the Western democratic capitalist countries and the unified élite which dominates the socialist societies, concentrating in the hands of a single group both economic and political power as well as a more or less total control over all forms of cultural expression.

Against such views of the total dominance of the élite in a new hierarchical form of society, in which perhaps a new type of class system emerged, it has sometimes been argued that at all events the ruling group had nothing, or very little, of a hereditary character about it, but was open and accessible to the whole population. The high rate of social mobility, and the absence of major barriers to mobility, were indeed often adduced as evidence that social classes (or relatively closed groups) were effectively disappearing in the socialist countries. A number of studies suggest, however, that, while overall mobility from manual to non-manual occupations does seem to be higher in the socialist countries, this may be largely attributable to the changing occupational structure resulting from industrialization (Heath, 1981, pp. 206–7). Again, mobility from manual worker origins into the élite has been particularly high in some socialist countries, and was undoubtedly encouraged by the policies of these regimes in the early post-revolutionary stages, but it was also facilitated by industrial development, and at a later stage the rate of mobility declined. Parkin (1971, p. 150–1) noted that in Eastern Europe the ruling communist parties underwent a long-term process of 'de-proletarianization', with a steadily increasing proportion of their members being drawn from a white-collar élite consisting of those with higher education who have technical and professional qualifications; and he concluded that 'the fact that the intelligentsia stands out as being socially and materially advantaged *and* so closely tied in with the Party would seem to reinforce the case for singling them out as a dominant class'. This is clearly very close to the argument later developed by Konrád and Szelényi (1979).

In any case, high rates of mobility do not signify the absence of classes; on the contrary, they presuppose the existence of a class structure (even if it is no more than a survival), but one which is relatively 'open' and may perhaps be gradually dissolved if there is a continued large-scale movement of individuals between occupations and social positions. More important, probably, in establishing some kind of 'classlessness' in the socialist countries was the upgrading of manual occupations, the tendency to reduce the cultural differences between social groups, and social policies designed to achieve equality of access to education, universal health care, full employment, low-cost housing, and a great range of public services in transport, recreation, and other spheres. Such measures, however, did not diminish the concentration of economic and political power, and the accumulation of privileges of all kinds, in the dominant group, which ruled these societies by repression and terror during the Stalinist period. From the 1950s, opposition groups emerged which began gradually to impose changes in the system, culminating in the massive upheavals of the late 1980s.

The first changes came in Yugoslavia, from 1950, with the introduction of workers' self-management on the basis of what was termed 'social ownership', as distinct from 'state ownership', of the means of production (Broekmeyer, 1970; Széll, 1988, pp. 104–11), and of socialist market relations among self-managed enterprises and between producers and consumers, within the framework of a central plan. For the first two decades the new system, which was continuously developed and modified, was very successful, both economically in achieving high rates of accumulation and growth, and politically in creating a society which was more open, democratic and 'classless' than any other in Eastern Europe, despite the absence of opposition parties. But according to the critics inside Yugoslavia, who became more numerous and outspoken from the 1970s as economic difficulties and political tensions increased, self-management had still been inadequately developed and there remained a gulf between the ruling group and the mass of the population. Thus, Stojanović (1973) and Golubović (1986) have both argued that what has so far been achieved in Yugoslavia is not a comprehensive system of self-management (or self-government) extending to the whole society, but a 'hybrid system' in which ' "social property" oscillates between state usage, which has no legal justification, and "group property" at the level of the enterprise as a visible form of the fragmentation of social property' (Golubović 1986, p. 23). The leading role of the League of Communists (the Yugoslav version of the Communist Party which was intended to signal the transformation of one-party rule into a 'non-party' system) means, according to Golubović (p. 36), that because of 'the retention (or renewal) of the characteristic relations of *domination* (of the political élite over other strata and individuals) and *exploitation* (in terms of the exclusive possibilities of a segment of society to decide on the use of the surplus product, depriving those who produce social values of the right to sovereign control over them), one can talk about the existence of a class society in Yugoslavia'. Hence the growing movement for a multi-party system, although this movement (as elsewhere in Eastern Europe) includes diverse interests, some of which seem intent upon re-establishing a capitalist class system. For socialists, on the other hand, the aim is to extend and make more effective – in conditions where there is no longer an immovable dominant élite – the practice of self-management, which for all its limitations and difficulties 'has survived and has shown its feasibility. It has proved that simple workers are able, without being experts, to run companies and institutions, and that this society therefore provides some hope that political apathy can be overcome' (Széll, 1988, p. 113).

Since the 1960s, numerous reform movements have emerged in other socialist countries, and by the end of the 1980s it was clear that in Eastern Europe, including the Soviet Union, political and economic institutions, and the class structure, were all in the melting pot (Bottomore, 1990). Some of the movements were influenced in their earlier stages by the Yugoslav system, but what they borrowed from it was mainly the idea of 'socialism with markets' rather than the project of self-management. Thus the New Economic Mechanism introduced in Hungary in 1968 substituted for direct central planning an indirect regulation of a more market-oriented economy, and was also more tolerant of private enterprise, which increased rapidly in the 'second economy' (Hare *et al.*, 1981). In varying degrees other socialist countries attenuated their 'command economies' and moved towards an indirect type of planning through financial and fiscal measures.

The reforms reached a culminating point at the end of 1989 when the political structures of the East European societies were rapidly transformed. These events throw light on the nature of the stratification system against which the revolts were directed. What all the movements contested was the political dictatorship of a self-perpetuating élite, and the absence of personal freedom – to travel, to express opinions, to criticize government policies or form a political opposition, to participate effectively in policy-making – so that the process as a whole can properly be described as a popular struggle for democratic rights, although dissatisfaction with the performance of the economy and with living standards contributed significantly to the intensity of the movements. From this aspect, therefore, the previously existing type of stratification can, it seems, be most appropriately conceived in terms of élite theory, as the domination of the whole population by a unified élite in a totalitarian system. It can be regarded as a class system, with a new ruling class, only if what is emphasized is the effective possession of the means of production rather than political power or the specific characteristics of a totalitarian system; but this ignores too many of the distinctive features of those societies, in which the social structure was indelibly stamped with Leninist, and still more Stalinist, conceptions and practices.

At the same time, as the studies I discussed earlier reveal, this stratification system, like the capitalist class structure, had various complexities and ambiguities, as well as some specific characteristics. There was, as Konrád and Szelényi observed, a steady increase in numbers of the 'intermediate strata', one part of which was no doubt closely aligned with the ruling group, while another part became increasingly involved in the opposition movements; and a more diverse array of social and political attitudes developed, as became manifest in the late 1980s. But there were also, in these societies, elements of 'classlessness', as several observers have pointed out, resulting from general social policies, the diminished importance of the manual/non-manual distinction, and the suppression by the ruling group of any associations in civil society which might formulate claims to a particular status by occupational or other groups. It is evident, I think, from all the various analyses of the socialist societies, that their stratification systems had several unique features which render direct comparisons with other types of society in respect of the class structure or the formation of élites inadequate, in spite of some significant resemblances. These societies have to be regarded, to a great extent, as being *sui generis*, and one particularly interesting and important question for historical–sociological study, now that a whole phase of their development has come to an end, concerns the processes and circumstances through which societies that embarked initially on a project of human liberation and equality ended as peculiarly repressive political dictatorships. Defenders of the Soviet regime portrayed the Stalinist period – during which the privileges of the upper stratum, political dictatorship, and rule by violence attained an extreme point – as a historical aberration, resulting from what came to be called the 'cult of personality'. But this is no explanation. The cult of personality has itself to be explained, and this is all the more necessary and urgent since its appearance contradicted all the expectations which Marxists and other socialists had about the nature of a classless society. An explanation might be attempted by stating the social conditions which are favourable to the rise of charismatic leaders, along the lines which Max Weber first suggested. In the particular instance of the USSR we could point to such features as the sudden break with the past in the revolution, and the stresses, together with the need for authority and discipline, engendered by the rapid industrialization of an economically backward country. Or else we may look for more general conditions which favour a unified élite, as Aron did when he argued that a 'classless society' (in the restricted sense of a society in which all economic enterprises are publicly owned and managed) necessarily produces a great concentration of power in the hands of the political and industrial leaders; and as Ossowski did when he suggested that political power had now become so important in all the industrial countries, but especially in the socialist countries, that the political élite was able to form and change the system of stratification rather than being itself a product of that system.

These ideas are quite at variance with Marx's conception of the relation between property ownership, social classes and political power, and also with his account of how the class system in modern societies would develop. The great extension of the activities of government, in economic development and in the provision of social services; the growth of highly organized and powerful political parties; the influence which can be exerted through the modern media of communication; these have all worked to establish a major division in society between the governing élite – which may include political and military leaders, high officials, and the directors of important economic enterprises – and the mass of the population, to some extent independently of social classes based upon property ownership or of other forms of stratification. In the USSR, where this division was most firmly established – because the political rulers belonged to a party, revolutionary in origin, which had an exceptionally rigorous organization, and which was further bound together by an all-embracing ideology – it was also most profoundly obscured, because the doctrine to which the ruling élite adhered excluded either recognition or investigation of such a phenomenon.

There is now, however, another major question arising from the sweeping changes that took place at the end of the 1980s; namely, how these societies will develop in the future, and what new kinds of social stratification are likely to emerge. It is still too early to predict in any detail or with any certainty the course of events, and there will undoubtedly be considerable differences between countries, but some major tendencies at least are already apparent. In Poland, the new regime is committed to the introduction not of a socialist market economy, but of a market economy *tout court*, to extensive privatization of enterprises, and to full integration in the capitalist world economy, signalled by the acceptance of loan conditions imposed by the International Monetary Fund. The first fruits of this policy have been massive price increases, a fall in living standards for most of the population, growing unemployment, and the emergence of soup kitchens to feed the hungry. Some of the worst effects may be alleviated, to some extent, in the longer term, but if the present policies are pursued without any restraint the end result will undoubtedly be a typically capitalist class system with great extremes of wealth and poverty. The trend in Hungary appears to be similar, although the new policies are perhaps being implemented more cautiously and gradually, and they are more organically connected with earlier reforms undertaken since 1968. The case of the German Democratic Republic is unique in that its future prospects are largely determined by an imminent reunification of Germany, the most likely outcome of which is the domination of East Germany by West German capital, the emergence of large-scale unemployment, and the reappearance of a capitalist class system. Nevertheless, there are several countervailing factors, and notably the strength of the reborn Social Democratic Party in East Germany and its close links with its powerful sister party in West Germany.

The situation in Yugoslavia and the Soviet Union is very different from that in the countries I have just considered. In Yugoslavia there is still a strong popular attachment to the system of self-management, but there are major disagreements between those who want to deal with the present economic and social problems by making that system more genuinely effective and those who want either to strengthen the apparatus of central planning or, on the contrary, to move more rapidly to a full-fledged market economy. The advent of a multi-party system, which is now envisaged, will make possible a direct and open advocacy of the diverse views, and it remains to be seen what the eventual outcome will be. At all events there is likely to be strong opposition to any fundamental changes in the system of social ownership and self-management. These issues, however, will be complicated, and in some cases perhaps overshadowed, by the growth of nationalist aspirations and movements, which are already prominent in Yugoslav politics and may obscure, in some cases, the problems of economic inequality and class structure.

In the Soviet Union, similarly, the social ownership of major productive resources seems not to be in question, and the present reforms envisage only changes (which are very important in themselves) in its character, from state ownership to various other forms of collective ownership or effective possession. Thus, a recent law concerning land ownership effectively transfers the ownership of land from the central state to the various republics, and provides for individuals to be small-scale owners, users, or leaseholders of land, while at the same time state and collective farms will continue, and will in fact become collective owners of the land they use. The law excludes a market in land, and hence the possibility that a new class of large landowners will develop. In the spheres of industry and trade similar changes are taking place, with the growth of small-scale individual or cooperative enterprises, and, most importantly, the decentralization of economic activity and decision-making from the state planning apparatus to socially owned enterprises – in which there may perhaps be in the future a larger element of self-management – operating in a 'socialist market economy' that is regulated indirectly at various levels within the framework of a general plan.[3] At the same time, there are projects for joint ventures with Western companies, the most noteworthy to date being the agreement with Fiat to expand and modernize car production.

The future course of these changes, and their eventual consequences for the class structure, cannot yet be clearly foreseen. Much depends upon the economic success of the policies of restructuring, and much also upon the political consequences of the gradual implementation of a multi-party system in which quite different, and conflicting, policies will emerge. Moreover, as in Yugoslavia, one of the first results of a more liberal and democratic political regime has been the vigorous growth of nationalist movements, whose doctrines and activities have little to do in many cases with economic modernization or the class system, and may be retrograde in their effects.

What is most evident in the recent history of the East European socialist countries is that the movements which swept away the political dictatorship of the Communist Party apparatus as the major element in the class or élite structure of these societies, were movements of the whole people for basic liberties and equal citizenship in a democratic system. In the Soviet Union and in Yugoslavia a more gradual process, in different circumstances, displays similar characteristics, complicated by nationalist aspirations, while in China the democratic movement has been, for the time being, violently suppressed. But once the elements of a democratic order have been achieved it soon becomes apparent that there are divergent interests and aims in this body of the whole 'people', closely related to the economic situation of different groups. The further these societies move towards a capitalist economy (and Poland is a notable example), the more likely it is that intense social conflicts based primarily upon class interests will reappear. However, some of the socialist countries may follow a different course, drawing more upon the experience of the Yugoslav self-management system or of cooperative production as it has developed in the Mondragon enterprise (Thomas and Logan,

1982), or on the example of the more 'socialistic' countries of Western Europe, and especially Sweden and Austria, rather than on models of a privatized free-market economy such as exists today in Britain (which is not conspicuously successful either economically or socially). The questions I have posed here raise larger issues concerning the political manifestations of class interest in the industrial countries at the end of the twentieth century, and they are more closely considered in the following chapter.

NOTES

1 A former socialist in Britain, in contrast, asserted that 'where there is no egalitarianism there is no socialism' (Jenkins, 1952).
2 See the definition of totalitarian regimes by Friedrich (1969) as characterized by a totalist ideology, a single party committed to this ideology, a fully developed secret police, and three kinds of monopolistic control – of mass communications, of operational weapons, and of all organizations, including economic ones.
3 I have discussed the different forms of social ownership and the relation between socialist planning and markets more fully in Bottomore (1990, chs 6 and 8).

4
Social Class, Politics and Culture

The egalitarian movement which came to life in socialist clubs, trade unions, cooperative ventures and utopian communities great stronger throughout the nineteenth century as capitalism developed. In the course of time this movement has taken many different forms – struggles for women's rights and against racial discrimination, and the efforts to close the gap between rich and poor nations – but its driving force remained the opposition to the hierarchy of social classes. The class system of the capitalist societies was seen as the very fount of inequality, from which arose the chief impediments to individual achievement and enjoyment, major conflicts within and between nations, and the political dominance of privileged minorities.

In this movement Marx's analysis of capitalist society acquired – directly or indirectly – a large influence, through the connections which it established between social classes and political institutions. According to Marx, the upper class in society – constituted by the owners of the principal means of production – is necessarily the *ruling* class; that is, it also controls the means of political domination: legislation, the courts, the administration, military force, and the agencies of intellectual persuasion. The other classes in society, which suffer in various ways under this domination, are the source of political opposition, of new social doctrines, and eventually of a new ruling class. Only in the modern capitalist societies, however, does a situation occur in which the contending classes are reduced to two clearly demarcated groups, one of which – the working class – because it contains no significant new social divisions within itself, espouses an egalitarian creed and engages in a political struggle to bring about a classless society.

The appeal of Marx's theory was twofold: it provided a clear and inspiring formulation of the aspirations of the working class, and at the same time it offered an explanation of the development of forms of society and government, and especially of the rise of the modern labour movement itself. When Marx undertook his studies, the class character of governments was very obvious in the European countries which had embarked upon industrialization. For much of the nineteenth century only property-owners in these societies enjoyed full political rights; and it was scarcely an exaggeration to conceive the government as 'a committee for managing the common affairs of the bourgeoisie as a whole'. In many European countries it was only during the first two decades of the twentieth century, and in some countries even later, that universal suffrage was finally established.

Since political democracy is such a recent growth, Marx can hardly be blamed for having failed to consider all its implications for the association between economic and political power. At least he did not disregard the importance of the suffrage. In an article in the *New York Daily Tribune* (25 August 1852), in which he discussed the political programme of the Chartists, he wrote: 'The carrying of Universal Suffrage in England would, therefore, be a far more socialistic measure than anything which has been honoured with that name on the Continent. Its inevitable result, here, is the *political supremacy of the working class*.'[1] On a later occasion, it is true, Marx (1871) referred in a more disparaging way to the right of 'deciding once in three or six years which member of the ruling class was to misrepresent the people in Parliament'. But he added immediately: 'On the other hand, nothing could be more foreign to the spirit of the Commune than to supersede universal suffrage by hierarchic investiture.'[2] The situations which called forth these divergent assessments were in fact very different. In the one case Marx was describing a state of affairs in which a working-class movement, organized on a large scale, would be capable of putting forward its own trusted candidates at elections; while in the other he was drawing a contrast between a government – the Commune – in which the working class could support candidates of its own, and a preceding condition in which it was able to vote only for one or another of the bourgeois parties.

From the end of the nineteenth century the creation and growth of mass working-class parties became a major factor in the political life of the more or less democratic European capitalist societies, gradually imposing more extensive social welfare programmes and other measures which tended to reduce the gap between rich and poor. The revolution in Russia, and the first attempt to create a socialist, classless society, stimulated the working-class movement throughout Europe, but it also divided it between the old socialist parties and the new communist parties, and this proved a fatal weakness in the 1920s and 1930s with the rise of fascism in Italy, Germany and Austria, and subsequently in Spain during the civil war.

At the end of the Second World War, however, after the defeat of the fascist powers, working-class parties in Western Europe – both socialist and communist – were stronger than they had ever been, and their influence also spread widely in the national liberation movements of colonial peoples in Asia and Africa, becoming still more potent for a time throughout the Third World after the revolution in China. In Western Europe, socialist parties, and briefly communist parties, had a major role in national governments, and the prospect emerged of a more or less rapid transformation of these societies in a socialist direction.

But the aspirations of the European working-class movement were checked by two major factors in the politics of the post-war world. The first was the overwhelming economic, political and military power of American capitalism, and the policies pursued by a society in which no significant socialist movement has existed since the early years of this century. In the United States, as I noted earlier, an egalitarian ideology derived from the conditions prevailing in the early nineteenth century – widespread small-property ownership, absence of a feudal past or of any collective historical memory of an aristocratic order of society, exceptional opportunities for geographical and social mobility – has persisted, notwithstanding the manifest class divisions in American society which emerged blatantly at the end of the century. This ideology of classlessness, although sometimes challenged (in the 1930s and again in the 1960s), has been powerful enough to inhibit the formation of an effective socialist movement. Several other factors have contributed to its success. Sombart, in an early study *Why is there no Socialism in the United States?* (1906), suggested as major influences the rising standard of living ('all socialist utopias have come to grief on roast beef and apple pie'), the social position of workers, the democratic style of public life, and the open frontiers. But there were also other influences, among which the situation of black Americans and the successive waves of immigration were particularly important. Black Americans formed a distinctive kind of American proletariat, with the lowest incomes, the most menial and subservient tasks, and the lowest social prestige (in part because of their slave origins) of any group in American society. The existence of this large, relatively homogeneous, easily identifiable, and exploited group meant that every white American, even the lowest-paid labourer, possessed a certain social prestige which raised him, at least in his own view, above the level of a proletarian. Immigration worked in much the same way to raise the social position of the ordinary American worker, since many groups of immigrants entered the lowest levels of the occupational hierarchy, and made it possible for those already established to advance themselves. But neither black Americans, nor any immigrant group, have contributed substantially to forming a proletariat in the sense that they have radically challenged the established order of society. And so, although the vigorous struggles of black Americans and other groups to gain full economic, civil and political rights (especially in the 1960s) may be likened to early class conflicts in Europe, in so far as these were concerned with the right to vote, with labour legislation and with social reform, they differ entirely from these conflicts to the extent that they aim exclusively at winning a place in the existing society and accept the predominant values of that society.

The absence of a strong socialist movement, for reasons which I have sketched above,[3] and the dominance of an ideology which stressed American 'exceptionalism' and some kind of 'non-egalitarian classlessness' (Ossowski, 1963, ch. 7), in which the quest for 'status' became pre-eminent,[4] made it

possible for the United States to establish itself as a bastion
against the spread of socialism in any form, and to intervene
actively all over the world (but particularly in Latin America) –
by economic pressure, internal subversion, or military intervention – in order to destroy any political regime which departed
too far from a capitalist form of society. In Europe, the growing
socialist movement after the Second World War was checked
partly by the Marshall Plan, involving large-scale economic aid
for reconstruction along capitalist lines (van der Pijl, 1989, pp.
252–8), but it also encountered a second formidable obstacle
in the expansion of Soviet communism in Eastern Europe.
The re-establishment, in the last years of Stalin's rule, of an
increasingly repressive political system, and the imposition of
harsh Stalinist regimes on the countries of Eastern Europe,
along with the existence in France and Italy of large communist
parties which, in the immediate post-war years, were more or
less totally subservient to Moscow (and remained so for a long
time in France), created an image of socialism which had very
little appeal for the working class in the democratic capitalist
societies, where in any case a combination of sustained economic growth and increased state expenditure on social welfare
had considerably improved its condition. Indeed, some sociologists took the radical view that the word 'socialism' had become
meaningless, except in reference to a family of authoritarian
states, and Touraine (1980, pp. 11–12) argued that:

> Socialism was the theory of the labour movement; in a
> large part of the world it has become the name of the
> state power [while] in other countries it amounts only to
> a defence of particular sectional interests which are less and
> less the bearers of a general project of human progress.

Notwithstanding these two great impediments – represented
on one side by American capitalism, and soon the rapid revival
of capitalism in Western Europe; and on the other by the
Stalinist, later authoritarian–bureaucratic, regimes in Eastern
Europe – the traditionally working-class and socialist parties in
Europe continued to grow in membership and influence during
the post-war period, although Britain was a major exception

in this respect (Bottomore, 1984b, ch. 11). The idea of a decline of working-class politics and of the socialist movement expressed by Touraine, and also by Hindess (1971), who argued that in Britain at any rate 'class polarization has declined markedly since the war and remains now only in touches of rhetoric to be produced on suitably solemn occasions . . . the Labour Party now appears to be less of a (working) class party than at any time in its history' (p. 10), was certainly exaggerated, although it might be claimed, as I did myself in the early 1970s, that class-based parties were being increasingly challenged by new political movements. At all events, the 1980s saw a fresh upsurge of the democratic socialist movement in Europe, accompanying the decline of American economic power and the dissolution of the communist autocracies.

At the end of the 1980s, socialist governments were in power in several European countries, and seemed likely to come to power in others, while in the parliament of the European Community socialists were by far the largest single group, and will probably form a majority in alliance with other left-wing groups, thus influencing significantly the social policies of the Community. The socialist parties continue to draw their main support from the working class, just as conservative parties are supported primarily by the capitalist class and by various sections of the middle class; and in that sense European politics is still unmistakably class based. But the extent to which class membership or class interest is explicitly or implicitly invoked in political campaigns and programmes, the nature and degree of class consciousness (and its variations between classes), and the actual content of political conceptions such as 'capitalism' and 'socialism', raise issues of great complexity which need to be analysed further.

Such an analysis has to begin from the fact that since the latter part of the nineteenth century class-based parties have dominated the political scene in capitalist countries, and still do so today. The major parties in these countries – conservative parties of various kinds on one side, socialist, communist, social democratic or labour parties on the other – are supported in the main by quite different classes, and their policies closely reflect different class interests: in the case of the former, ensuring maximum scope for the activities of private capital, limiting public ownership and public expenditure to the greatest degree that is compatible with the maintenance of a minimum level of social peace and adequate electoral support, and keeping taxation of high incomes and of capital gains to the lowest possible level; in the case of the latter, maintaining a high level of public expenditure on the social infrastructure and social services, favouring public ownership in some spheres (and to varying degrees), creating instruments for (mainly indirect) economic planning and the regulation of market forces, and using the tax system as a means of reducing the most blatant inequalities of wealth and income.

What then has changed in the politics of social classes in the post-war era? We can best approach this question by considering first the political orientation and influence of particular classes. There is now a substantial literature in the social sciences which argues that it is no longer possible to define clearly a capitalist class that dominates the economy, and still less one which is a quasi-permanent 'ruling class'. The argument has several strands: the control of the economy is no longer wholly or even mainly in the hands of the owners of capital, but is exercised to an increasing extent by professional managers, or what Abercrombie and Urry call a 'service class' (see above, page 45); the privileges of aristocratic and other wealthy families have been eroded by the generalization of a 'meritocratic' system of recruitment to important positions; and the development of democracy has made it impossible for a single class to monopolize political power. In spite of their wide diffusion and acceptance, these arguments are not very securely based. Many studies have shown that inherited family wealth continues to dominate the economy, and is a principal basis for the recruitment of managers even in this supposedly meritocratic age.[5] In general, the important managers in large corporations also own substantial amounts of capital. The question of capitalist class rule in a democracy is more complex. On the one hand, democratic political systems and the growth of socialist parties, which have intermittently (or for a long period in the case of Sweden) been in power, have limited the direct and unconstrained rule of this class, which has now to appeal to a wider electorate and to compete with other powerful political movements. Similarly, the extension of public ownership and increase in public spending restrict the area in which the capitalist accumulation process can operate. These observations refer primarily to Western Europe, much less to Japan (although the socialist party there is now becoming a stronger political opposition), and only in a very weak sense to the United States, which remains quite exceptional for reasons discussed earlier.

On the other hand, in spite of these changes, the capitalist class in Western Europe, and still more in Japan and the United States, has retained its dominant position in society. Pro-capitalist governments have predominated in the post-war period, and the class as a whole has unmistakably succeeded in retaining, and even increasing, its wealth and its effective control of the economy (Bottomore and Brym, 1989). The question we have to consider is how this general dominance has been sustained in conditions of political democracy, and in the face of strong socialist movements.

The first relevant factor is the specific capacity of the capitalist class to act collectively in defence of its interests. The notion of 'collective actors' is itself a difficult and contested concept, especially in its application to classes (Hindess, 1987, ch. 7, and 1988, ch. 4), and we have to recognize at all events that such 'actors' are very complex social entities.[6] The actions of classes, in particular, present great analytical difficulties (though similar problems arise, for example, in studying 'national interests' and the actions of nations); and there are quite evidently great variations, in different historical and national contexts as well as between different classes, in the capacity to act collectively. What can be argued, however, is that there are many favourable circumstances which tend to make the capitalist class a more effective collective actor than other classes. One of these is the fact that it constitutes something like an 'organized minority' in Mosca's sense, in which there is a relatively high degree of interaction among the members through family connections, similar educational backgrounds, interlocking directorates, business associations and so on; from which emerges a highly developed class consciousness and a very clear awareness of class interests. Another circumstance is that the capitalist class possesses or controls ample resources (economic and cultural) for coordinating action and implementing decisions. These resources also give it a great advantage in influencing public opinion and determining the general framework of ideas and assumptions within which social and political debate will take place, since the crucial mass media are for the most part, and increasingly, owned by large capitalist corporations.

The capitalist class can no longer rule by limiting the suffrage as in the nineteenth century, nor is it necessary in ordinary circumstances to rely upon coercion, although there have been plenty of instances, at various times in the twentieth century, of coercive rule through fascist or military dictatorships, of the use of force on a more limited scale against trade union and radical movements, and of military intervention against anti-capitalist regimes (above all by the United States). For the most part, in the post-war democratic societies, domination by the capitalist class has been assured mainly by what Gramsci called 'hegemony' (Gramsci, 1929–35, especially pp. 55–60; Sassoon, 1983); that is to say, by gaining the allegiance, or at least the passive consent, of a majority of the governed, which has involved making some compromises while still protecting the vital interests of the class. Hence the acceptance of increased public expenditure, the welfare state and even some elements of a 'mixed' public and private economy. Nevertheless, the capitalist class will consistently try to limit the extent of such developments, and in favourable circumstances will conduct a counter-offensive to reduce public spending, extend the sphere of capital accumulation by privatizing state corporations, and diminish what is laughably referred to as the 'burden of taxation' on the rich. This kind of 'class struggle from above' was a salient feature of politics in Britain during the 1980s.

It is not easy, however, to rule by hegemonic means, as the present difficulties of capitalist societies – and notably Britain – show. There are significant divisions within the capitalist class itself in some countries,[7] and these, together with the divergent economic and social interests of various social groups, particularly in the middle class, which normally support capitalist rule, may engender major differences in policy, so that government action becomes confused and unsure. At the same time there is a persistent pressure on the capitalist class by other classes, which tends to limit its power, and in some historical circumstances – such as the upheavals of war or a major economic depression – may severely curtail it. In so far as the capitalist class has been able to maintain its dominant position during the post-war period, therefore, one major factor has been the weakness of opposing, or potentially opposing classes, and especially the working class. This weakness is to be understood, however, only in a relative sense. As I indicated earlier, working-class parties, in Europe particularly, have generally increased their membership and their electoral support since the war, socialist governments have been in power at various times (and almost continuously in Sweden), and in the late 1980s socialist parties became a dominant force in the European parliament. The weakness consists in the fact that socialist governments have not been able to gain or retain the allegiance of a substantial majority of the population in the major capitalist countries over long periods of time, or to bring about fundamental changes in the economy and the structure of society. Moreover, working-class parties have tended to become increasingly reformist in many cases, to abandon their more ambitious aims of creating a 'new civilization', and to eliminate from their doctrines and programmes any explicit reference to the conflict of class interests. One of the earliest and clearest indications of this tendency is to be found in the programme adopted by the German Social Democratic Party at its conference in Bad Godesberg in 1959, which shed its long Marxist tradition and excluded any mention of 'class' or 'class struggle'.

Many factors have influenced this evolution of working-class politics. One of these, unquestionably, was the horrific example of the Stalinist 'socialist' regimes in the Soviet Union and Eastern Europe, which discredited, by association, not only the idea of socialism but also Marxist thought as one of its vital elements. But there were other factors internal to the development of capitalist societies, which I have referred to previously: the diminishing size (in relative, and later absolute, terms) of the manual working class; rising standards of living which resulted from economic growth, full employment (until the 1970s), and the expansion of social welfare policies; and a modest redistribution of wealth and income through the tax system. All these factors, internal and external, tended to retard the development of a distinctive class consciousness in the working class and to diminish its political role; so that socialist parties everywhere had to look for additional support in other social groups, and in many cases thought it necessary, in order to attract that support, to moderate, or even exclude, any reference to class interests or the ultimate aims of socialism in their programmes.

It is important, however, not to exaggerate these changes in working-class politics. There never was a 'golden age' in which the working class solidly supported socialist parties or when those parties themselves were united in their conceptions of socialism and the ways in which it might be attained. On the contrary, it has been evident throughout the twentieth century that 'nowhere has *socialist* consciousness taken hold of the entire working class' (Hilferding, 1941), and that where a socialist consciousness did exist it was nevertheless often divided between different parties and movements whose conflicts with each other sometimes had tragic consequences, notably in Germany in the 1920s and 1930s, and in the Spanish civil war. In 1945, socialist parties in many European countries, and communist parties in some countries, were stronger than they had ever been in terms of membership and electoral support, and this strength has been largely responsible, through its influence on policy-making, for the greater prosperity and sustained economic growth of the whole post-war period. But it has never been quite enough to present a radical challenge to the dominance of the capitalist class, or to accomplish a decisive movement from an advanced form of the welfare state (such as exists in Sweden, for example) to a predominantly socialist form of society.

Although working-class parties for the most part have retained their popular support and their political influence, with some fluctuations over time and considerable variations between countries, they have also had to adapt themselves to the new economic and social circumstances which they helped to bring about, and in particular to the decline in the size of the working class (above all in the older industries – coal-mining, iron and steel, railways – which had formed the core of the traditional labour movement) and the growth of the middle class, which came to be seen as a crucial factor in political life, or even as the dominant force in constituting a new kind of 'middle-class' society and culture. In fact, however, the political orientations and actions of the middle class are extremely diverse and changeable, and this reflects in large part its great heterogeneity as a class. No specifically middle-class party has ever succeeded in establishing itself as an important political actor, although particular sections of the middle class have sometimes briefly become a political force, as in the case of the Poujardist movement of small shopkeepers and artisans in France in the early 1950s. More generally, liberal and centre parties have been largely supported by sections of the middle class, but such parties have never had a major role in the class politics of the post-war period, and their influence has been significant mainly in situations where coalition governments had to be formed because neither conservative nor socialist parties had an overall parliamentary majority. In recent years, also, this role of liberal parties has been taken over in some cases by new political groups such as the green parties, or by the surviving communist parties (much diminished in membership and electoral support), in a few countries.

The heterogeneity of the middle class is very evident, and so great indeed that many social scientists have questioned the pertinence of regarding it as a single class, preferring instead to refer to 'middle classes' or 'intermediate strata', whose place in society is defined only by the fact that they do not form part of either the capitalist class or the working class but are situated precisely 'in the middle' or 'in between'. The diverse categories or strata in the middle class can be distinguished along many different lines: in terms of educational qualifications, style of life, work situation, property ownership, and various combinations of these elements. Middle-class persons may be highly qualified professional people (Johnson, 1972) or routine clerical workers (Lockwood, 1958). They may constitute a petty bourgeoisie of small entrepreneurs and the

self-employed (Bechhofer and Elliott, 1981, ch. 8); they may
be employees, at various levels of skill and responsibility, in
public or private corporations, in the civil service, in teaching,
or in social welfare agencies. These different sections of the
middle class are categories rather than social groups, although
organized groups may develop within them (e.g. professional
associations and white-collar trade unions); and the political
orientations of the middle class, while they are influenced by
the particular location of different categories in the social structure – by levels of property ownership and income, work situation, and educational qualifications – as well as by membership
of professional bodies and trade unions, are extremely variable
within as well as between categories. There is a well-known
phenomenon of 'middle-class radicalism' (Parkin, 1968), and
the social movements of recent times – the peace movement,
the green movement, feminism – have originated in middle-
class milieux and drawn their members largely from the middle
class. Equally, however, middle-class individuals and groups
have sometimes provided strong support for fascist regimes or
military dictatorships. On other occasions important sections of
the middle class have acted as a liberal, even 'permissive', force
in social life,[8] through the arts and literature, and through their
involvement in movements of social reform, and have searched
for a third way between capitalism and socialism, or for some
form of 'capitalism with a human face'. But it can certainly not
be claimed that the middle class, or the intermediate strata,
have been consistently an element making for stability and
liberalism in the political order. On the contrary, their political
attitudes and actions are extremely mutable, vacillating and
diverse, and the growth of the middle class has been one important factor in the instability and fluctuations of economic and
social policy in most of the capitalist countries since the war.

This instability has not, however, undermined the general
dominance of the capitalist class, but has mainly affected the
politics of the working-class movement. One consequence of the
expansion of the middle class has been to create for a substantial
part of the population a great variety of differentiated social
situations, which appear to form a continuum of more or less
clearly defined status positions, determined by a variety of

factors and not simply by property ownership. This implies a different conception of the social hierarchy as a system of stratification by status rather than a class system in which there are fundamental class conflicts. This middle-class view of the social structure, as we may broadly call it, has been widely diffused, not only in the social sciences, but in the general social consciousness, and its diffusion has played some part in the gradual erosion, if not the abandonment, of class politics in the actions of many working-class parties. Whether this erosion was bound to take place in any case, for other reasons, and how precisely it occurred, are difficult historical questions which remain unsettled. In spite of the growth of the middle class, the working class still forms a large part (close to 50 per cent) of the population, and an effective mobilization of its support would have given socialist parties long periods in power, as in Sweden, where social democratic policies themselves have created a greater awareness of class differences and more clearly defined class voting (Scase, 1977, Conclusions). The influence of a large middle class on working-class politics may be further questioned if we take into consideration the arguments about the 'deskilling' and 'proletarianization' of sections of the middle class (Braverman, 1974), or about the emergence of a 'new working class' which includes technicians and research workers who challenge in various ways the capitalist organization of production (Mallet, 1975).

Such arguments, however, have been the subject of much dispute.[9] It seems clear that the technological advances and the increasing differentiation of occupations in modern societies – with which the growth of the middle class is associated – have in fact made the formation of large class collectivities more difficult (though this is less true in the case of the capitalist class, for reasons discussed earlier). But the formation of such collectivities, or of what Marx called a 'class for itself', is also influenced by other factors, and notably by the development of political parties themselves, in a wider context of cultural and social movements. As Max Weber (1921) argued, classes 'are not communities; they merely represent possible, and frequent, bases for communal action', and in considering the present-day class system as a whole, the main issue to be resolved is how far, and with what consequences, these possibilities for communal action have changed and are continuing to change. This theme will be taken up in the next chapter, in relation to changing economic and political conditions, and the rise of new social movements.

First, however, we have to consider how the class structure, or the distinctive type of social stratification, that existed in the socialist countries of Eastern Europe has evolved. A process of reform began soon after Stalin's death in 1953, involving a gradual relaxation of direct central planning, and a mitigation of the harshness of political repression; but more radical projects of reform were suppressed and the communist parties retained their monopoly of political power. From the late 1960s, however, the pace of reform increased, and it accelerated again after 1985 when profound changes were initiated in the Soviet Union. Up to that time, the main thrust of the reforms had been to achieve a decentralization of economic decision-making by introducing elements of a controlled 'socialist market economy' (such as had been developed in Yugoslavia since 1950) and modifying the system of central planning, which moved gradually from a 'command' mechanism to one relying more upon indirect and 'indicative' controls (Bottomore, 1990, ch. 6). These changes themselves tended to diminish the power of the central planners and communist party officials – that is to say, of the dominant 'class' or ruling 'élite' in the socialist societies – and hence to create a greater fluidity in the class system.

These tendencies were reinforced by another feature of the reforms, which introduced a greater 'openness' (*glasnost*) into social life, thereby encouraging a rapid growth of public criticism of the regimes. During 1989 the tide of criticism swelled, and the demands for economic reform were associated with demands for political democracy, an end to the communist monopoly of power, and the restoration of a multi-party system. By the end of the year, popular mass movements for democracy had overwhelmed the old regimes in most of the East European countries, and the whole social structure of these societies was quite clearly in the melting pot. Their future development is still uncertain, but it is already apparent that there are considerable differences between countries, and that the new class system will not take the same form in every case.

In Poland and Hungary the aim of the new regimes appears to be a more or less complete restoration of capitalism, through privatization and the establishment of a free-market economy. Hence, in these countries what is most likely to emerge in the short term is a new class system virtually identical to that in Western Europe. In a different way a similar outcome appears likely in East Germany, where the process of German reunification may well lead to domination by West German capital and a reprivatization of a large part of the economy. Here, however, there are stronger forces opposing the restoration of capitalism, and in the elections of March 1990 the conservative alliance failed to obtain an absolute majority of votes, or of seats in the new parliament, while the Social Democratic Party and the reconstructed communist party (Party of Democratic Socialism) together obtained 38 per cent of the votes and thus constitute the nucleus of a substantial opposition. The situation in other socialist countries – Bulgaria, Czechoslovakia, and Romania – was less clear in the spring of 1990, but socialist parties and reconstructed communist parties still appear to have considerable support. In Yugoslavia it is also unclear whether the rapid extension of a market economy by the present government and the institution of a multi-party regime will radically undermine the self-management system; but in this case nationalist movements and the conflicts among the constituent republics are a major complicating factor.

The case of the Soviet Union is very different in that there is as yet no major challenge to the socialist economy, and therefore very little prospect in the short or medium term of a reinstatement of capitalist class relations. So far at any rate it is a socialist market economy which is being developed, with an emphasis on greater enterprise autonomy, indirect central, regional and local planning, encouragement of cooperative production, a modest expansion of private production and trade in some spheres. The new law on property approved by the Soviet parliament in March 1990 decentralized the control of land use to the constituent and autonomous republics, established limited rights to own, lease and inherit land (while excluding a market in land), and also permitted individual ownership of small businesses as well as some hiring of employees, though this is strictly regulated. Socially owned property will remain the dominant element in the economy, and in this sense the society will continue to be 'classless'. What has changed, and is still changing with the gradual development of a multi-party system and a more distinct separation of power between party and state, is the absolute dominance of the Communist Party and the bureaucracy over the whole of Soviet life. From this process there may emerge a form of democratic socialism in which there is no domination either by a capitalist class or by any other privileged group – party officials, bureaucrats, 'rational redistributors', or whatever they may be called – and in that case the Soviet Union would become more effectively a classless society than it has ever been.

In all the socialist countries the accelerating process of change has been affected by several different factors. One of these, which has been operative throughout, is the steady increase in numbers of the middle class or intermediate strata – the well-educated professional, technical and administrative personnel – upon whose work economic development in particular crucially depended. This large segment of the population, constituting in a broad sense an intelligentsia (whose importance is emphasized by Konrád and Szelényi, 1979, ch. 13), although its interests were to some extent bound up with those of the ruling group, had nevertheless a strong interest in economic and political reforms which would create opportunities for personal initiative and innovation, greater economic efficiency, and a more liberal political regime in which critical debate about social policies and problems could take place. In the event this intelligentsia played a prominent role in the radical reform movements (beginning in Hungary in 1956 and Czechoslovakia in 1968) and was strongly supported by other sections of the population, notably by urban workers.

However, the success of the reform movements also depended crucially upon two other factors. The first was the complex of economic problems which emerged in the late 1960s, when it became clear that the system of highly centralized command planning, which had been effective in the earlier period of massive industrialization and post-war reconstruction, no longer functioned so well in a mature economy affected by increasingly rapid technological change and the proliferation of new consumer wants. Out of this situation arose the preoccupation with the 'scientific–technological revolution' and its social implications (Richta, 1969), and the first tentative movement (outside Yugoslavia) towards 'socialism with markets'. The concern with economic performance, the changing structure of production, and the diminishing confidence in the ability of the ruling group to improve conditions then produced a widespread movement for greater personal freedom and more extensive democratic participation, for the kind of 'socialism with a human face' that was briefly expressed in the Prague Spring of 1968. This popular democratic movement eventually became the most powerful force in transforming the European socialist countries.

What forms of class structure or classlessness will emerge in the long term from these upheavals can as yet be only speculatively conceived, but it is already clear that, in the short term at least, there will be considerable differences between countries in respect of the new economic and social order which they attempt to construct and their success in doing so. In most countries, however, in the early stages it seems likely that distinct social classes, and class politics, will reappear, as is already evident from the results of the first elections; but at the same time there are other social movements, particularly nationalist movements, often closely connected with religious faiths, which will have an important role in political life (as they already do in the Soviet Union and Yugoslavia). In all the industrial countries, therefore, whether their past experience is that of capitalism or socialism (in their diverse forms), the political conflicts of the near future will involve not only classes but also an array of collectivities and communities whose consciousness of kind – resulting from ethnic, national, linguistic, cultural, or other affinities – may engender, in some circumstances, social movements which affect the balance of power in society and the character of social change. In the next chapter I shall consider how far this more diversified social scene has changed the role of social classes themselves.

NOTES

1 This article was conspicuously omitted from earlier editions of the official communist collection of Marx and Engels' writing on Britain, but was eventually included in the 1962 edition.

2 How uncomfortable Marx would have been, if indeed he had survived at all, in the socialist societies of Eastern Europe which invoked his name, where 'hierarchic investiture' was precisely the method used to appoint the people's rulers.

3 For a more comprehensive account, and diverse evaluations of the phenomenon, see Weinstein (1967), and Laslett and Lipset (1974). I have also discussed some other aspects of American radicalism, in the context of the social movements of the 1960s, in Bottomore (1967).

4 Hofstadter (1963) made a distinction between 'class politics' and 'status politics' and argued that in the United States the basis for the latter is broader and stronger than elsewhere because of the 'rootlessness and heterogeneity of American life, and above all, of its peculiar scramble for status and its peculiar search for secure identity' (p. 83); a scramble and search that are in turn explained by the massive immigration between 1881 and 1920, which exacerbated the struggle to 'belong', to acquire or retain a recognized status.

5 See Bottomore and Brym (1989) and the references given there. Some earlier studies in the USA (W. Miller, 1962; Baltzell, 1962) showed, for various periods, and notwithstanding the supposed 'classlessness' of American society, that the leading positions in the economic system were occupied predominantly by individuals recruited from old-established business and upper-class families. As to meritocratic recruitment in general, it should be observed that individuals from wealthy families have every advantage (in respect of access to education and social connections, as well as stocks of capital) in entering top managerial positions. The prescient comment by Émile Boutmy, founder of the *École libre des Sciences politiques* in Paris as an institution for the education and recruitment of a new administrative élite drawn from the upper class, is worth noting here:

> Privilege has gone, democracy cannot be halted. The higher classes, as they call themselves, are obliged to acknowledge the right of the majority, and they can only maintain their political dominance by invoking the right of the most capable. . . . The tide of democracy must encounter a second line of defence, constructed of manifest and useful abilities, of superior qualities whose prestige cannot be gainsaid. (Letter of 25 February 1871)

For a recent study of how this process works in the recruitment of business leaders through management schools, see Marceau (1989).

6 This question is examined more fully in Bottomore (1975, chs 6, 7).

7 See the studies of individual countries in Bottomore and Brym (1989), and in particular the case of Italy (pp. 109–39).

8 Leonard Woolf once responded to a question about the social influence of the Bloomsbury Group by saying that it had helped to create the 'permissive society'. That is perhaps a mixed blessing, and in any event less important than the creation of a society of equals.

9 They are criticized, for example, by Abercrombie and Urry (1983, pp. 55–60), and by Mann (1973, ch. 7). See also, for an analysis of some important differences between French and British workers, Gallie (1978).

5
The Future
of Social Classes

First we must look to the past. From the mid-nineteenth century to the mid-twentieth century two kinds of conflict dominated world politics. One was the class conflict between bourgeoisie and working class, which became steadily more intense from the last two decades of the nineteenth century to the 1930s. The other was international conflict, partly the colonial wars of capitalist nation states, partly the conflicts among those nation states themselves to maintain or expand their empires.

These two forms of conflict were related in various ways. First, in the view of many scholars (Bauer, 1907; Braudel, 1972; Kohn, 1967; Tilly, 1975) the development of modern nation states was closely associated with the rise of the bourgeoisie and the expansion of capitalism, and, as I have argued elsewhere (Bottomore, 1979, ch. 5), 'modern nationalism can be seen as one aspect of a class movement'. Secondly, however, nationalism came to be seen at a later stage, by Marxist social scientists in particular, as a doctrine and social movement which was inimical to the development of the working-class movement. The Austro-Marxists, who confronted both the problems of nationalism in the multi-national Habsburg empire and the expansionism of Imperial Germany, undertook major studies of the national question and of imperialism[1] in relation to the working-class movement (Bauer, 1907; Hilferding, 1910; Renner, 1917). The intensity of nationalist–imperialist feeling was shown clearly by the initial popular enthusiasm for the First World War, and the inability of the working-class movement in any country to prevent its outbreak or, for a long time, to arouse any widespread opposition to it.

After 1945, however, the character of international conflict changed radically. Colonial wars gave way to wars of national liberation, and the conflicts between imperialist states were transmuted into more peaceful and regulated economic competition and a supranational capitalist domination of a large part of the Third World, initially under the leadership of the United States. The principal source of international conflict then became the division between two major groups of countries, one described as socialist or totalitarian, the other as capitalist or democratic, depending upon the theoretical and ideological standpoint of the observer. These changes have had substantial, multiform and in some respects contradictory effects upon class politics, interpreted in diverse ways, some of which I have briefly considered in earlier chapters. We have now to examine, in a historical context which includes the most recent transformations of the East European societies, the modes in which these consequences may prolong themselves in the medium-term future.

I shall begin by analysing the situation of the principal classes in the industrial societies. The capitalist class is immensely more wealthy and powerful than it has ever been, and its power will be further increased by the restoration of capitalism which now seems probable in some of the East European countries. There are several reasons, mentioned earlier, for this accession of strength in the post-war period: greater stability, population growth, more extensive state regulation of the economy and a degree of economic planning, the expansion of welfare services, which provide some kind of minimum standard of living (and hence sustain demand), the rapid growth of credit, major technological innovations which gave a periodic stimulus to the economy, and massive military expenditure. Until the 1980s, therefore, capitalism appeared to be highly successful (notwithstanding some shocks during the 1970s) in its various forms of welfare capitalism or a social market economy, and it showed few symptoms of the decline that Schumpeter (1942) had diagnosed as probable. But this high summer of post-war capitalism seemed to be drawing to a close as problems accumulated in the late 1980s, although the opening up of Eastern Europe may provide some temporary relief. A variety of difficulties now confront capitalist regimes: high unemployment, inflation, a slowing of population growth and the prospect of a declining population in some countries, ageing populations which make greater demands on welfare services, an inadequate flow of savings to finance necessary investment resulting in high interest rates, and in general a stagnation of the economy (more marked in some countries, such as Britain, than in others) which may well become a recession, along with increasing conflict between the rich and the poor.

In the face of these difficulties, however, the capitalist class, for reasons discussed earlier, remains immensely powerful and still has a dominant influence on economic, political and cultural development. But its continued dominance is not assured and the eventual outcome depends upon the strength of opposing forces, and in the first place on the future orientation and actions of the working class and its organizations. It is a notable feature of the post-war situation that, while the capitalist class became stronger and in some respects still more effectively organized, especially at an international level (van der Pijl, 1989), so too did the working class in many capitalist countries, above all in Europe. Trade unions generally increased their membership and their influence up to the late 1970s, as did socialist parties in many countries, and this growing power was a major factor in the development of welfare states.[2] Thus a degree of unity of working-class action was achieved during the post-war period (more effectively indeed than in earlier periods) in spite of the difficulties that have always arisen, and have frequently been noted by social scientists, from the differentiation within the working class itself between skilled, semi-skilled and unskilled workers, between employed and unemployed workers, between those in different sectors of the economy.[3] Such unity, however, was much more difficult to achieve on an international scale, and in particular there remained throughout the post-war period a profound ideological division between the socialist parties in capitalist countries and the communist parties that held exclusive power in the socialist countries. But this situation has begun to change radically, with the transformation of the socialist countries into multi-party regimes, and the growing possibilities for coordinated socialist action in the European Community, so that a broadly European alliance of working-class parties seems an increasingly realistic prospect for the future.

Whether there is such a development depends, however, upon several other conditions. In the first place, we have to consider how the working class is at present constituted, and in what ways its numbers and its social and political attitudes are likely to evolve in the medium-term future. The question of the boundaries of the working class as a distinct social group has long been a matter of controversy among Marxists and between various schools of Marxist thought and their critics. Undoubtedly its core consisted of manual industrial workers, and, as Przeworski (1977, p. 354) observed, 'In 1848 one simply knew who were the proletarians. One knew because all the criteria – the relation to the means of production, manual character of labor, productive employment, poverty, and degradation – all coincided to provide a consistent image.' But this situation had already changed by the end of the nineteenth century, and still more in the second half of the twentieth century. Przeworski (pp. 355–6) cites a Soviet definition in 1958 of the proletariat as 'the class of people separated from the means of production, having therefore to live from the sale of their labour power to the owners of capital and exploited in the process of capitalist production', and goes on to note that 'this definition includes secretaries and executives, nurses and corporate lawyers, teachers and policemen, computer operators and executive directors'. The heterogeneity of the working class defined in this way is even greater than that suggested by studies of differentiation within a more traditionally conceived working class, and although there are some points of connection, for instance with the idea of a labour aristocracy (see note 3), the definition leads mainly to the more familiar recent problems and controversies concerning the expansion of the middle class and the related decline of the working class.

If, notwithstanding these changes, socialist parties which have their historical basis in the working class have become stronger in the post-war period, this may be explained in various ways. It may be argued that some sections of the middle class –

and in particular the low-paid white-collar employees – have become increasingly aware that they are in fact workers, whose conditions of life and work are not very different from those of many groups of industrial manual workers, while other middle-class employees in state educational and welfare services have developed a commitment to the welfare state which brings them closer to the social doctrines of working-class parties. This corresponds with the view of Marxist thinkers from Kautsky to Renner (1953), the latter arguing that the 'service class' is now 'closer to the rising working class in its life style, and at its boundary tends to merge with it', and to recent writers. That some such process has been occurring is confirmed by the growth of white-collar trade unionism, especially in the public services, and during some periods the increasing militancy and radicalism of these unions.

However, the increasing strength of socialist parties can also be explained in another way; namely, by the adaptation of socialist doctrine, aims, and policies in order to attract greater support from sections of the middle class. This change is apparent since the 1950s in the programmes of many social-ist parties, which have eliminated references to class politics, become more hesitant about public ownership, and tended to concentrate their attention almost entirely on immediate issues of welfare policy. Whether these developments have in fact been responsible for their increasing electoral support is not clear. It is arguable that if the socialist parties had retained more of their traditional orientation, and had concentrated their efforts upon gaining a larger share of the core working-class vote (a significant part of which always went to conservative and liberal parties), they would have been even more successful, not only because they would have had more solid working-class support and a larger proportion of votes at every election, but because the manifest strength of their electoral support among at least one half of the population would have had a powerful influence upon the politics of some sections of the middle class. Indeed, two European countries – Austria and Sweden – where the socialist parties have to a large extent retained their traditional aims show just how successful this alternative path can be.

Against this view, however, it may also be argued that the working class (as I discussed earlier) has itself been changing in conditions of greater prosperity and economic security, resulting from welfare services and full employment (until the 1970s), and would not have responded to traditional, more distinctively socialist doctrines. This is now less clear, as insecurity increases again, but the argument raises issues of more general scope which are crucially important in considering the future of class politics. Unlike the capitalist class, which has only to defend *existing* interests (of property in general and capital in particular) and needs to resort to an explicitly formulated social doctrine (frequently in terms of the organic development of some postulated 'tradition', as in Hayek's later writings) only when its domination appears to be seriously threatened, the working class has the much more difficult task of constructing, through trade union, cooperative and political organizations, a conception of an alternative *future* form of society without class domination. Historically, Marx's theory of capitalist development and the rise of the working-class movement has been the principal source of ideas about the nature of a socialist society and how it is to be attained; and it has had a profound impact on political action over the past century, not only through explicitly Marxist parties but also more diffusely through its influence on other strands of socialist thought and practice. But Marxism itself became divided into opposing schools with very different theoretical and political views, while in the working-class movement as a whole a great variety of doctrines flourished, from anarchism and syndicalism to Fabian socialism and Bolshevism. What is more, as many observers always recognized, a socialist consciousness of any kind had never taken hold of the entire working class.

The question today, and for the future, is what the content of a socialist consciousness is, or might be,[4] and whether there is still, in some stronger or weaker sense, an elective affinity between the working class and socialism. This raises the most difficult problems of 'class interest' and 'class consciousness'. It has sometimes been argued (most recently by Hindess, 1989, especially ch. 5) that class interest cannot be objectively determined and that classes are not 'collective actors' pursuing such interests through political action. In some respects this renews in a different form the arguments of some earlier writers to the effect that the socialist movement was largely the creation of dissatisfied intellectuals. Thus Machajski (1905) expounded the theory that socialism expressed the ideology of such intellectuals, and that its attainment would result, not in a classless society, but in the establishment of a new ruling class in a system which he characterized as 'state capitalism'. Schumpeter (1942) also saw the intellectuals, increasingly hostile to capitalism, as 'invading' labour politics, radicalizing it and 'eventually imparting a revolutionary bias to the most bourgeois trade union practices' (p. 154). Such arguments form a curious counterpart to Lenin's view of socialism being brought to the working-class movement 'from outside', by revolutionary intellectuals.

But this complex of arguments has several weaknesses. First, it should be noted that attention is focused upon the working class, and that, for example, Hindess's rejection of this idea of 'objective interests' does not refer at all to the capitalist class, where the identification of such interests does not seem insuperably difficult. Furthermore, it needs to be considered more thoroughly whether the description and analysis of class interests in general is inherently more questionable than that of national interests, which are regularly invoked in political doctrines and in social theories (for example by Max Weber), or of numerous other kinds of specific 'interest'.[5] The main argument against objective working-class interests is itself difficult to reconcile with the historical development of the labour movement. No one can seriously suppose that this movement sprang into life simply from the imaginations of disaffected intellectuals, like Athena from the head of Zeus, although bourgeois thinkers (and Marx foremost among them) played an important part in defining and expressing its aims, and especially in analysing the the structure of the existing capitalist society in which its struggles take place. What is most evident in this history is the interaction (characteristic of all social life) between the experienced wants and interests of a large collectivity, and the efforts of intellectuals to comprehend more clearly the implications of those interests, out of which the modern working class emerged as a quasi-group (Bottomore, 1987, ch. 6) which constitutes (in Weber's terms) an enduring basis for communal action and does in fact, in particular situations, generate large-scale group action.

To be sure, it may be argued that the most immediately experienced wants and recognized interests of workers are those concerning wages and conditions of work, which involve trade union action rather than a political commitment to socialism. Nevertheless, these two forms of working-class action were closely allied from the beginning, and developed even closer links, not solely through the intervention of intellectuals, but in large measure spontaneously. A more difficult question, especially in present circumstances and for the medium-term future, concerns the nature of that commitment to socialism, and this involves the broader issue of how socialism as an alternative form of society is now envisaged. There was always some uncertainty, and much controversy, about the organization of a socialist economy as the basis of a new society (Bottomore, 1990, Introduction and chs 1 and 2), but the context of these debates has changed radically in the post-war period as a result of economic growth and more widespread prosperity in capitalist countries, and still more the experience of totalitarian–authoritarian socialism in the Soviet Union and Eastern Europe. The upheavals in Eastern Europe at the end of 1989 have created conditions there in which, for the time being and quite understandably, a general distaste for socialism and hostility towards the whole socialist idea are widely expressed, and in some countries (notably Poland) there is a determination to restore capitalism as quickly as possible. In the West, as was noted earlier, the idea of socialism has also been changing and it is no longer at all clear in many countries what the aims of socialist parties are, beyond a commitment to the improvement of social welfare provision, and in particular what degree of attachment there is to public ownership and planning, which have hitherto been considered essential distinguishing features of socialism.

The future role of the working class will therefore depend not only on its changed social and economic situation, which I examined earlier, but even more on a restatement of the aims and policies of the socialist movement that effectively connects these with the more immediately experienced concerns and wants of workers, in the conditions created by the increasing instability of capitalism which emerged during the 1980s. In this future development the growth of the middle class seems likely to have rather less importance than is sometimes attributed to it. As I have argued, independent middle-class parties rarely become large or coherent enough to have a decisive political influence. For the most part, the middle class divides its allegiance between the two major class parties: the upper echelons, who have high incomes, a certain amount of property, relatively independent working conditions, and a role in the economy which involves some of the functions of managing capital and controlling the labour process, support pro-capitalist parties; while the middle and lower strata, who experience greater insecurity, own little property, have incomes not much higher (and in some cases lower) than those of industrial workers, and whose living standards are much more affected by the level of public educational and welfare provision, are more inclined, either consistently or in particular circumstances, to vote for socialist parties. But it is also a notable characteristic of middle-class politics that there are considerable fluctuations in allegiance, whereas the major class parties retain over long periods a solid core of support.

In recent years one of the most important manifestations of middle-class politics is to be found in its involvement in what are called the 'new social movements', which have frequently been regarded as marking a significant shift away from class politics. These movements – the student movement, feminism, the anti-nuclear and peace movements, the environmental movement – rose to prominence in the late 1960s, and many of them have continued to develop since then, predominantly supported by members of the middle class. Other movements, ethnic or nationalist (sometimes inspired by religious zeal, and in a few cases tinged with racism), have rather a different character and will be considered separately, as will the pro-democracy movements which burst into life in Eastern Europe and in China during 1989.

But how 'new' are these social movements? It should be remembered that the labour movement itself was a social movement manifesting itself in Chartism, in revolutionary upheavals and sporadic riots, and in other forms, before there were organized working-class parties or any major development of trade union organization, and that even now it retains something of the character of a broad movement. Throughout the nineteenth and twentieth centuries, many other social movements also flourished, from anti-slavery campaigns, anti-war movements, student movements of diverse orientations, to the suffragettes, and we have to consider not only whether (and, if so, in what ways) the more recent movements differ from their predecessors, but also how they are likely to evolve, particularly in relation to social classes and political parties.[6] One of the most sustained attempts to interpret the significance of recent social movements, incorporating the results of a wide-ranging project of research on particular movements, is that of Touraine (1971, 1977, 1981, 1987), who emphasizes 'action' rather than 'structure' in his analysis of modern societies, which he conceives as having reached a stage in which there is a 'self-production of society' through the conscious, deliberate intervention of diverse social groups and movements. At the same time, however, he defines social movements as 'the organized collective behaviour of a class actor' (1981, p. 77), although classes themselves are no longer defined by their location in an economic and social structure (the ownership or non-ownership of property), but are more vaguely conceived in terms of domination and subordination expressed in political and cultural contestation. Furthermore, he also argues (1987, p. 214), in what appears a somewhat contradictory way, that 'what remains of the labour movement' (i.e. a class movement in the Marxist sense, which emerged directly from the economic and social structures of capitalism) 'is still the strongest example of a social movement that can be observed in our type of society'.

Probably the most significant aspect of the recent growth of social movements is the contribution they make to an extension of democracy beyond the sphere of parties and elections, in a process which can be represented (along with various forms of industrial democracy and self-management, which are at least as important) as a further stage in the 'self-production' of society or along the road to 'participatory democracy'. The social movements, however, may advance towards their goals in various ways: by critical opposition or resistance to specific public policies and institutional arrangements; by influencing more generally government legislation and the programmes of political parties; by bringing about changes in consciousness, in cultural and social conceptions, among some sections of the population; or in some cases, where their aims involve a more comprehensive reconstruction of society, by forming new parties, as the environmental movement has done. In the latter case, particularly, we need to look more closely at the relationship with existing class parties. Undoubtedly, the green parties are non-class parties, in the sense that they do not appeal for support to a particular class, and notwithstanding the fact that they are largely the creation of middle-class groups; but because of the nature of their aims and policies they are close in many respects to the socialist parties, with which, in recent years, they have formed various kinds of alliance in West Germany and in the European Community. The other major social movements – the student movement in the 1960s, feminism, and the peace movement – have also been close to socialist parties and to the socialist movement in its various forms, and it may be argued that the movements (as was also the case in earlier times) have in fact brought an accession of strength to parties whose main support comes from the working class, while at the same time modifying and adding new dimensions to their policies. This is not to say, however, that the social movements or the parties which they may sometimes engender will be, or should be, absorbed into existing working-class parties. On the contrary, flourishing social movements of the kind I have so far discussed would be a vital element in the extension of democracy, and the eventual achievement of what both Marxists and liberal thinkers used to describe as a 'self-directing humanity', in any conceivable socialist commonwealth of the future.

The case of ethnic and nationalist movements is very different. Ethnic minorities within nation states may create social movements or organized associations to campaign for equal citizenship and/or the recognition of special cultural needs, and in situations where most of their members are also economically deprived they are likely to ally themselves with working-class parties, although even in this case they may still aspire to a distinctive status, as the advocacy of 'black sections' within the British Labour Party indicates. At the same time, the presence of ethnic minorities and their growth in Western Europe as a result of post-war immigration have also led to the emergence of strongly nationalist, neo-fascist counter-movements, which have become more prominent in conditions of economic recession and high unemployment.

But ethnic groups themselves may constitute the basis of nationalist movements where their aims go beyond the acquisition of full citizenship rights and become claims to complete independence or at the least to a high degree of autonomy within a very weak form of federal state or confederation. There were elements of such nationalism in the American Black Power movement of the 1960s (Cruse, 1967), while in Quebec during the same period a powerful independence movement developed which has recently revived again. In Western Europe, nationalist movements, varying in the degree of their radicalism or moderation, have emerged or renewed themselves in several countries: in Belgium, in Spain (notably in the Basque country, but also in claims for greater autonomy in Catalonia), in the UK (in Northern Ireland and Scotland). Where nationalism does emerge strongly, either in separatist movements within existing states, as a response by the nation state to such movements, or in the form of counter-movements against what is seen as a threat to national identity resulting from the cultural diversity introduced by immigrants, it does evidently tend to eclipse class politics, although the relationship is a complex one. As I noted earlier, the creation of nation states in Western Europe was closely connected with the rise of the bourgeoisie and the development of capitalism, and nationalism has always been an important element in the politics of conservative parties, whereas socialist parties have generally emphasized internationalism and have often been anti-militarist. In other parts of the world, in more recent times, however, nationalism has sometimes been a broader populist movement – as in the nationalist movements in the Habsburg Empire, the national liberation movements in colonial territories, and movements inspired by religious fundamentalism of one sort or another in the Middle East – and in these cases it may for a time quite overshadow class divisions.

The most recent manifestation of the power of nationalism in a reaction against previously existing conditions is to be seen in Eastern Europe. The movements against the Bolshevik dictatorship in these countries, which became steadily more powerful in the late 1980s, were above all pro-democracy movements, committed to multi-party politics and to economic reforms, and it was possible to envisage their outcome as a transition to a regime of democratic socialism with markets. This is still the prospect in the USSR, and perhaps less clearly in Yugoslavia, but in some of the other countries since the end of 1989 the new regimes have adopted policies which involve a full-scale restoration of capitalism. At the same time, very strong nationalist sentiments have emerged which serve to bind together ideologically the members of societies that are passing through traumatic experiences of reconstruction and reorientation, and in some sections of the population these sentiments have assumed extreme forms in hostility to minority groups, anti-Semitism and neo-fascism.[7] In the Soviet Union (which is a union of constituent republics) and in Yugoslavia (which is a federation of republics) nationalist agitation and separatist movements have become exceptionally important, obscuring to some extent, and diverting resources from, the efforts to bring about political and economic reforms which would ensure the development of a democratic socialist order. The nationalist movements everywhere are in most cases conservative and traditionalist, and in Poland, Hungary and Czechoslovakia they are closely linked with the aim of re-establishing a capitalist economy. In East Germany the elections of March 1990 became virtually a plebiscite on the question of the reunification of Germany, and the issue of independent development as a socialist society was completely submerged, so that here also a restoration of capitalism, dominated by West German capital, seems inescapable in the near future.

The nationalist movements and the return to capitalism are comprehensible to a great extent as a reaction against four

decades (and longer in the Soviet Union) of experience of autocratic, Stalinist and neo-Stalinist regimes which fatally tainted
the whole idea of socialism. But nationalism and neo-capitalism
will produce new divisions and conflicts, or restore earlier ones,
and in those revived capitalist societies class politics will also
revive. The transformation of the East European societies,
therefore, does not, any more than does the development of
welfare capitalism or organized capitalism, put an end to the
major political role of class-based parties, but reintroduces all
the problems and conflicts that spring from inequalities of
wealth and income, class domination, economic fluctuations
and insecurity, and widespread unemployment.

What it does do, however, is to pose serious problems for the
Marxist theory of history, in which the idea of a reverse movement from socialism to capitalism has no place. This theory –
which for more than a century has been the principal ideological
inspiration, directly or indirectly, of working-class politics – has
therefore either to be abandoned, as has happened throughout
Eastern Europe in an understandable reaction against decades
of forced indoctrination, intellectual charlatanry, Stalinist sav-
agery and the subsequent dull compulsion of bureaucratic regulation, or to be radically reconstructed. The danger inherent in
the latter course, as in the revision of all theoretical schemes,
is that the theory may be made so flexible and accommodating
as to approach vacuity; for example, by displacing the transition to socialism into some remote inaccessible future while
regarding all intervening changes as minor events which do not
fundamentally affect the onward march of history. This would
reproduce two elements which were clearly present in Marx's
own thought: a utopian vision of the future socialist society,
and more importantly the Hegelian residue, transposed from
a spiritual to a naturalistic plane, of an underlying conception
of some historical *telos*. But the main content of Marx's work
was a realistic analysis of the origins of capitalism and its later
development, of the rise of the working-class movement, and
of the growing conflict between classes, and it is this kind of
analysis which still needs to be pursued in new conditions, as
has indeed been begun by some Marxists during the last two
decades.

Two distinct sets of circumstances confront such an analysis. The first is that prevailing in the capitalist countries, where, as I have argued, class-based parties are still pre-eminent in political life, and both the capitalist class and the working class, in different ways and degrees, have tended to become stronger and more effectively organized. But the capitalist class has remained economically and socially dominant, and the gains made by working-class parties have been intermittent and limited in most countries, due in part to uncertainties about the content and meaning of socialism (reflected in their programmes and policies) which arise from experience of the problems of socialism itself (Bottomore, 1990, ch. 7), but also in part to the growth of social movements – particularly the green movement and feminism – which raise issues that are quite distinct from those of class inequality. Undoubtedly, there is now a larger sphere of non-class politics, even though most of the social movements tend to be close, in some aspects of their policies, to socialist parties. On the other side, the gradual 'socialization of the economy' (which the Austro-Marxists and Schumpeter, following Marx himself, regarded as a major determinant of the 'march into socialism') has continued unabated in the post-war period, through the massive expansion of capitalist corporations, and through steadily increasing state regulation of the economy; and the latter at least has been an important factor in strengthening the position of socialist parties. But these parties have still to work out in new terms the relationship between public ownership, planning, and a socialist market system, especially on a supranational level in such organizations as the European Community.

The other situation that requires a new realistic analysis is that of Eastern Europe following the collapse of the Bolshevik regimes. There, as I have indicated, there is at present widespread disillusionment with socialism (and especially with Marxist conceptions of it), although circumstances differ very greatly from one country to another. In some countries – Poland, Hungary and East Germany (which is, however, a special case) – there is not only a resurgence of nationalism, but also a strong commitment to the restoration of a capitalist market economy. This process, however, is already creating familiar class oppositions, which are likely to intensify as the problems and costs of capitalism become more apparent. In Czechoslovakia the opposition of interests is already evident between those who desire a rapid privatization of the economy and the introduction of a free-market system, and those whose aim is rather to bring about more gradual reforms in which a large part of the substance of a socialist economy would be preserved; while in Bulgaria the former communist party, reconstructed as the Bulgarian Socialist Party, has considerable popular support and will probably have a major influence on the future development of the economy in a socialist direction. In the Soviet Union, the question of private ownership has not yet become a major issue, but there is conflict between different groups over the extent and nature of a market system (and its relation to socialism), as also over the degree and conditions in which investment by foreign capitalist corporations should be permitted or encouraged. In the immediate future, however, the political situation is likely to be dominated by the growth of nationalist movements, and this is also the case in Yugoslavia, where there is, however, a very clear opposition between those who want to preserve and develop the system of social ownership and self-management, and those whose aim is a radical transformation of the economy into a free-market system.

The present condition of the East European countries is one of great confusion and uncertainty, in which very diverse outcomes are possible, and it does not fit easily, or at all, with Marxist conceptions of the emergence and development of socialist society. The Marxist theory may certainly be reconstructed in such a way as to recognize that the rise of the working class, and the movement towards socialism, is an altogether more protracted affair than Marx ever supposed, experiencing many setbacks in its course, but that is by no means a sufficiently radical revision. As I have argued elsewhere (Bottomore, 1984b, pp. 189–90), 'we have to give up entirely that element in Marxism, and in some other socialist theories, which conceives the transition from capitalism to socialism as a historical necessity. Socialism is only a *possible* future'.[8] How 'possible' it is depends upon a great variety of factors. The restoration, or partial restoration, of capitalism in parts of Eastern Europe will at the same time revive class politics, as is indeed already happening, and the great modern conflict of capitalism versus socialism will be revived throughout Europe, and in different forms in other areas of the world.

But the character of this conflict has changed profoundly. No sudden revolutionary transformation is in the least likely to occur in any advanced capitalist country, and the major revolutionary upheavals of recent times have in fact been those in the autocratic state socialist societies. For the future the conflict will no doubt continue on the same course that it has followed in Western Europe since the war, in what the Austro-Marxists described as a 'slow revolution', proceeding by democratic means and aiming to bring about cumulative changes in the economy and in social institutions. When Otto Bauer (1924) wrote, in criticism of the Soviet dictatorship, that 'no government, whatever its dictatorial powers, can lead a capitalist economic organization to socialism unless there are first strong and mature social organizations which are organic to it, and which have been developed in the free and democratic activity of the masses', his view was remarkably close to that expressed by Sidney Webb (1931, p. 32) in his argument that 'important organic changes can only be . . . democratic, and thus acceptable to a majority of the people, and prepared for in the minds of all . . . gradual, and thus causing no dislocation, however rapid may be the rate of progress', and such ideas have been strongly reasserted in the doctrines of socialist, and communist, parties in recent years.

From this standpoint the recent changes in Eastern Europe, and especially the creation of 'strong and mature social organizations', can be seen as part of the slow revolution, restoring the vital connection between the working-class movement and the democratic movement which the Bolshevik dictatorship had destroyed. Whatever the immediate consequences of the current reconstruction of these societies, the process of gradual cumulative change (which does not exclude some specific major reforms or innovations) is likely soon to be resumed. In Western Europe, the democratic class struggle in the post-war period has brought important gains for the working class in the shape of improved living and working conditions and more extensive social services, even though the dominance of the capitalist class has continued relatively unimpaired; and this struggle continues, more clearly defined in some countries than in others. The socialist parties in Austria and Sweden, for example, aim to extend social welfare and to achieve a progressive democratization of society by increasing the participation of workers in the management of industry; in West Germany to develop the 'social market economy' in the interests of workers; and in the European Community to implement the project for a 'social charter' in such a way as to attain a more democratically organized economy.

How far this slow revolution will proceed, and over what span of time, it is impossible to foresee in any detail. In a democratic process of change everything depends upon the ability to mobilize support for specific short-term policies as well as more distant social ideals, and there are in present-day capitalist societies many circumstances (in addition to greater prosperity and more adequate social welfare) which may make it more difficult for socialist parties to retain, consistently and over long periods, the allegiance of a large majority of the working class, or to gain the support of other social groups and movements. Thus, the growth of leisure time encourages to some extent a withdrawal into private life as a consumer; at the same time it provides a partial escape from, and compensation for, the subordination experienced in the labour process, just as, in another way, does the increase in self-employment which has accompanied the more recent development of the service sector of the economy. Hence the work situation, and collective action in relation to it, may become less important as a determinant of working-class consciousness.

Several studies undertaken in the 1950s already drew attention to these changes. Zweig (1961, p. 134), in his study of workers in four modern enterprises, observed that 'when speaking about classes a man would seem to be thinking primarily about himself, about the individual aspect of the problem, and not about the social situation or the social structure', and went on to say that, although two-thirds of the workers he interviewed placed themselves in the working class, this recognition of their *class identity* was not accompanied by any strong feeling of *class allegiance*. A study of French workers by Andrieux and Lignon (1960) arrived at very similar conclusions. The authors distinguished three types of reaction among factory workers to their situation in the economy and in society: (1) evasion (the attempt to escape from industrial work either by rising to a higher position within the firm or by setting up in business on one's own account); (2) resignation (a dull and resentful acceptance of industrial work as an inescapable fate); and (3) revolt (opposition and resistance to the capitalist organization of industry). Of these three types, the second was by far the most common, while the third was the least so; and even the 9 per cent of workers in this category, who believed that they could improve their situation by collective action, no longer believed that any future society would be able to alter fundamentally the subordinate position of the worker in the factory. The authors summarized their results by saying that, although the workers they studied still had a group consciousness (i.e. they regarded themselves as 'workers', clearly distinguished from other groups in the population), they no longer had any collective aims. The present-day worker is 'a man who is cut off from working-class traditions and who possesses no general principles, no world-view, which might give a direction to his life' (p. 189). This conclusion, they observed, agreed entirely with those reached in a number of studies in Germany, by Popitz, Bednarik and others. Popitz (1957) and his collaborators, in their study of workers in the Ruhr steel industry, showed that there was a strong working-class consciousness, built around the distinction between manual workers and those who plan, direct and command work; but that those who still thought in Marxist terms of the victory of the working class and the attainment of a classless society were a small minority. Similarly, Bednarik (1953) concluded his essay on the young worker of today by saying that 'society has ceased to be an ideal for the working class', and that the worker 'tends more and more to withdraw into private life' (pp. 138–9, 141).

Several of these ideas were brought together by Goldthorpe and Lockwood (1963) in their analysis of the notion of embourgeoisement (see above, pages 19–20), where they suggested that there had been some convergence between the 'new middle class' and the 'new working class', leading to a distinctive view of society which diverges both from the radical individualism of the old middle class and from the comprehensive collectivism of the old working class. In this new social perspective collectivism is widely accepted as a means (and this accounts for the spread of trade unionism among white-collar workers), but no longer as an end (which accounts for the weakening of class allegiance among workers). Goldthorpe and Lockwood used the terms 'instrumental collectivism' and 'family centredness' to describe the complex of beliefs and attitudes in this conception of society. The latter term refers to the phenomenon which other writers described as a withdrawal into private life, revealed, in their view, in individual workers' predominant concern with their family's standard of living, their own prospects of advancement, the education of their children and their opportunities to enter superior occupations.

It was, no doubt, considerations of this kind which led many of the socialist parties in Western Europe to expunge references to class and class politics from their programmes, and to modify their proposals for extending public ownership. But in the decades since the 1950s it is not at all clear that the retreat into private life and the abandonment of collective aims by the working class, or by sections of the middle class, has made any significant progress. Indeed, this whole conception is contradicted by the development of more 'socialistic' countries such as Sweden and Austria, the successful extension of public ownership in France since 1981, the increasing political demands for greater industrial democracy, and the rise of the new social movements.[9] Several factors have been important here.

First, as Mallet (1975) suggested in his study of the 'new working class' (see above, page 20–1), because workers as producers are still dominated and constrained, while as consumers they experience a new freedom and independence, it is in relation to the working environment that class consciousness is most vigorously expressed. This is apparent, he argued, in the changing nature of trade union demands in the modern sectors of industry, which are concerned increasingly with shorter hours of work, longer holidays, and greater control over the policies of management. The painful contrast between work and leisure[10] is also evident from the comments reported by Andrieux and Lignon (1960). Workers mentioned frequently and bitterly the difference in the treatment which they receive from other people according to whether they are recognized as workers (in the factory, travelling to work) or as citizens (in leisure time). One worker summed it up by saying that as a worker he was pushed around, but 'when I am out in my car and stop to ask for directions the policeman comes up touching his cap because he thinks he is dealing with a gentleman' (pp. 31–2). Many later studies (Fraser, 1968, 1969; Terkel, 1974; Beynon, 1984) have depicted in a similar way the constraining and frustrating nature of industrial work, and of much clerical work, which continues to fuel the collective demands, not only for greater leisure, but for a different organization of the labour process.

It is hard to conceive that this division between work and leisure can persist unchanged, but it may be overcome or mitigated in several different ways. Continued economic growth might eventually result in such a reduction of working time (shorter hours, longer holidays, later entry into work and earlier retirement) and consequent expansion of leisure time that the hierarchical and authoritarian structure of production comes to play a negligible part in the individual's personal and social life, and is no longer a matter of overriding concern. On the other hand, there may be renewed efforts to introduce into the sphere of economic production some of the freedom and independence which exist in leisure time, and these efforts may be helped by changes in the character of production itself, as it becomes increasingly a scientific activity – using both the natural and the social sciences – which needs the services of highly educated and responsible individuals to carry it on. Most probably, there will be some combination of these two movements; but in so far as the second one takes place at all it will be through the actions of working-class organizations seeking to control the labour process, which is, in the Marxist view, the fundamental activity and form of social relationship in every human society, and always in some degree, however ameliorated, a realm of necessity.

A second influence which has a continuing importance in the European societies comes from the post-war extension, and more general acceptance, of public ownership of some basic industries, of state regulation of thee economy, and of public provision of a wide range of social and cultural services. The sharp contrast between 'private opulence' and 'public squalor' (Galbraith, 1958) has awakened many people to the fact that in a modern industrial society many of the most valuable private amenities can only be got or preserved through public action. A majority of individuals may be able to provide more or less adequately for their personal needs in food, housing, transport, and some kinds of leisure activities, but they cannot individually assure what is needed for full enjoyment in the way of a high level of education and health care, travel (through a planned transport system), facilities for sport and recreation, good working conditions, or a congenial and attractive urban environment. On the contrary, the unrestricted pursuit of private wealth and private enjoyment leads to the impoverishment of these vital public services, as the experience of Britain during the 1980s most graphically illustrates.

The policies of working-class parties have played a major role in the extension of public provision and national planning, and in Western Europe they continue to do so, in an increasingly vigorous way, in some individual countries and in the European Community. In much of Eastern Europe, on the other hand, the first fruits of the overthrow of one-party rule have been a widespread rejection of socialism and class politics, and a resurgence of nationalism, but in the longer term, as I have argued, class parties of the West European type are likely to re-emerge strongly, and indeed already exist incipiently. What is most questionable, however, in the economic and social conditions of the late twentieth century, is the significance that public ownership and economic planning will have in the confrontations between classes. The capitalist class, to be sure, will continue to defend, and so far as possible enlarge, its property and its control of the labour process, but it will also continue to make concessions, as it has done throughout the post-war period, in respect of limited planning, a degree of public ownership and state intervention in the economy, and the provision of welfare services, in so far as these are necessary to ensure social stability and the successful operation of the capitalist economy itself. In short, it will accept, in most countries, some version of a 'mixed economy', depending upon the nature of the mixture.

The middle class, divided into various categories by diverse economic and social situations, will no doubt continue to be divided in its political allegiance, but as a whole does not show any strong commitment to policies which would extend public ownership or economic planning, although there are important differences between countries; in France, for example, a *dirigiste* tradition seems still to have a significant influence. It is in the politics of the working class, however, that these issues have become most crucial. In the classical definitions of socialism, as the doctrine of working-class parties, two central conceptions were those of social ownership and a planned economy;[11] but it is no longer clear today what place these conceptions occupy in the policies of such parties, or what significance they have in the consciousness of workers. At all events, there are at present few signs of great enthusiasm for any substantial extension of social ownership in the capitalist countries – although the existing degree of such ownership is widely accepted in Western Europe, while in the exceptional case of Britain the privatization policies of the past decade have been strongly opposed – and in Eastern Europe the policies of some of the new regimes seem to envisage a large-scale conversion of socially owned enterprises into private companies and corporations. These attitudes have been reflected in – but may also have been reinforced by – the changing policies and programmes of socialist parties, in which the idea of social ownership has now, in many cases, an inconspicuous, scarcely visible place.

The idea of planning seems to have met a similar fate. The experience of centralized planning in the socialist countries has associated it with the authoritarianism of one-party rule, while in the capitalist world any extension of planning evokes fears of excessive regulation and bureaucratic inertia. Beyond this, the problems of planning in a technologically advanced, very diverse, and rapidly changing modern economy have raised

doubts about its efficiency as a method of organizing production. Such considerations have largely overshadowed the
real achievements of planned economies, especially in bringing
about rapid industrialization, as well as the success of partial
planning in the more 'socialistic' West European countries.[12]

Socialist parties have, I think, succumbed too easily to the
criticisms of social ownership and economic planning, and have
correspondingly neglected fundamental criticisms of the operation of capitalist economies. At all events, the consequence of
these changing attitudes has been that the opposition between
classes is now less clearly defined politically. In particular,
those parties which were historically working-class, socialist
parties now, for the most part, occupy positions which imply
an amelioration of capitalism and a more developed form of
welfare state – 'capitalism with a human face' – rather than any
radical reconstruction of society. In some European countries,
and in some parties, it is true, the process of reform is seen
as a cumulative one, which will eventually lead to a more
recognizably socialist and 'classless' society – and that is, I
think, a realistic outlook in the circumstances of the present
time. In many cases, however, there is no such long-term view,
and in so far as the basic structure of a capitalist economy
is accepted then, in the absence of any profound crisis, the
strength of the capitalist class will continue to increase.

The present situation of classes in the West European countries, resulting from the post-war growth of socialist parties, the
development of social welfare services, and economic growth
(sustained until the end of the 1970s) in predominantly capitalist economies, modified in varying degrees by elements of a
'mixed economy' and greatly increased public spending, might
be described as one in which the populations of these societies
are roughly equally divided between those who desire to extend,
at least in a modest degree, the socialization of the economy
(in the sense of more social ownership and a more planned
economy) and those who wish to maintain an existing form
of mixed, but primarily capitalist, economy, or to change the
mixture towards a more *laissez-faire*, free-market system. This
balance of forces, which some studies of advanced capitalism
(e.g. Habermas, 1973) have interpreted in terms of a 'class

compromise' reached during the period of very rapid economic growth in the 1950s and 1960s, found expression in a kind of 'consensus politics' – neither capitalist nor socialist, but fluctuating between expansion or contraction of public welfare services and between opposed views on fiscal policy which would alter the distribution of wealth and income between classes. Whether this is a stable balance in conditions of slower economic growth, large-scale unemployment, and perhaps less rapid technological innovation, remains to be seen. In the 1980s it has been more frequently disturbed, on one side by the offensives of the capitalist class against high levels of public expenditure and any extension of social ownership, on the other side by working-class demands for higher wages, shorter working hours, and improved welfare services. But the latter do not amount to a demand for 'socialism', largely because the idea of socialism itself has become unclear in the doctrines of socialist parties themselves. The future of class politics depends crucially, therefore, upon a rethinking of socialism, especially in the light of experience of authoritarian socialism and its collapse, but also more positively in a reconsideration of diverse forms of public ownership, and of possible combinations of socialist planning with markets.[13]

The scene is further complicated, however, by the development of new conceptions and forms of political action, some of which I have discussed above. In an earlier work (1971), reprinted in Bottomore, 1975, pp. 114–31) I noted that a new style of politics had become apparent in four principal directions: the rise of new élites committed to rationality and efficiency in production and administration, and subscribing wholeheartedly to the doctrines of technological progress and unlimited economic growth; the growth of radical movements which directly oppose the technocratic and bureaucratic character of modern industrial societies, and advocate 'participation' and 'community' as alternatives to the authoritarianism and élitism implied in the conception of a society directed by experts; the emergence of regional and nationalist movements; and, at the other pole, the growth of movements to create supranational communities, best exemplified in the European Community. All these styles, distinct from class politics, flourish today, and are likely to do so for the foreseeable future. The role of élites characterized by technological and administrative competence has a central importance in political debate in conditions where a major universal aspiration is for high living standards throughout society. Such élites, however, can in principle play the same part in a socialist as in a capitalist society, though in the context of different views concerning universal welfare. But the conception of a society managed by experts that is inherent in some of these ideas is still, and increasingly, challenged by those – and notably today the green movements and parties – who emphasize the problems created by technological advance and unrestrained growth as well as the undemocratic character of technocracy and bureaucracy when they are not subject to political debate and control. The third style of politics, regionalism and nationalism, also continues to flourish, and has received a new impetus from the collapse of the state socialist regimes in Eastern Europe, while acquiring a more menacing character with the emergence of neo-fascist movements in Europe, both East and West, though still on a small scale. Finally, the European Community has gained a new lease of life with the movements towards a unified market and some eventual form of political union, and especially with the prospect of a closer association with Eastern Europe, the resuscitation of the idea of a distinctive Central European culture, and the discussions about a common 'European homeland'.

These diverse alternative political concerns may diminish the centrality of class politics, and in any event impinge upon them. Equally, however, class politics have an important influence on other forms of political action, as can be seen from the division between conservatives and socialists on many issues in the European parliament, the various alliances between green and socialist parties in West Germany and in the European Community generally, and the frequently conservative or traditionalist character of nationalist movements. But there is, in this *fin de siècle*, a confusion of images of the future. The demands, by individuals and groups, for greater equality in economic and social conditions and for more democracy, especially in the sense of greater participation in all the processes of 'producing society', are still strong. But how are such demands to be satisfied? The experience of socialist countries has demonstrated that the road to a 'classless' society is neither direct nor smooth, and that new classes or élites, as well as dictatorial regimes, can well emerge along the route. So it has become relatively easier to present the advantages of a dynamic and democratic capitalism, in spite of its gross inequalities and economic uncertainties; and correspondingly more difficult to outline, in terms appropriate to the present time, the structure of a new kind of society. The opposition of class interests in capitalist societies – between the owners of capital and the propertyless, the powerful and the subordinate, 'those who live in light and those who live in darkness' – no longer manifests itself so plainly in class conflict, and the future political expression of these interests will depend more crucially than before on the ways in which the alternative to capitalism is conceived, and then implemented in a gradual process, through critical debate and in the light of experience of different policies. Above all, this is necessary with respect to the economic structure of a socialist society.

NOTES

1 Renner (1917) argued that in the era of finance capitalism the old principle of 'the unity, freedom and self-determination of the nation' had been replaced by the dominant idea of 'national imperialism' promoted by the ruling classes.

2 A study of seventeen advanced capitalist states by O'Connor and Brym (1988) shows 'that the more highly organized working classes are in trade unions, the greater the degree to which (a) left parties gain long-term cabinet participation, and (b) corporatist structures are created for societal-level tripartite bargaining among unions, capitalist umbrella organizations and the state. In turn the establishment of mechanisms for societal-level bargaining is associated with increased state intervention as reflected in more welfare spending' (cited in Brym, 1989, pp. 197–8). Brym (1989, pp. 198–9) also shows how increasing working-class power in Canada between 1945 and 1981 encouraged the expansion of health and education services, unemployment insurance, and regional development programmes.

3 Max Adler (1933), in a study of the working-class movement after its defeat by fascism in Italy and Germany, argued that

'the present-day proletariat is riddled with such economic conflicts – and an associated profound ideological alienation of various sections of the proletariat from each other – that it is doubtful whether we can speak of a single class'. He went on to distinguish five separate strata in the working class which had given rise to three different political orientations, of 'the so-called labour aristocracy and bureaucracy, of the proletarians who are employed, and finally, of the unemployed'. The idea of an 'aristocracy of labour' was widely discussed from the mid-nineteenth century onwards (Hobsbawm, 1964; Bottomore, 1983), and in a different form emerged in Michels' (1911) analysis of oligarchy in working-class political parties and in the more recent debates about embourgeoisement.

4 I have discussed this more fully in Bottomore (1990, ch. 8).

5 These issues are more extensively analysed in Benton's (1981) critical study of 'interests' as an essentially contested conception.

6 For a more extensive discussion of the 'new social movements', see Scott (1990), who similarly questions the validity of a rigid distinction between 'old' and 'new' movements and also notes (ch. 5) that there are strong incentives for a movement which wants to carry on large-scale, long-term activities to create a formal organization and eventually, in favourable circumstances, to become a political party, as is exemplified particularly by the formation of the Green Party in West Germany.

7 See the essay by Konrád (1990), who suggests as a solution to some of these problems the creation of a Central European federation. The problems of such a federation, however, in the context of long historical traditions of national diversity and hostility, are very great (Ash, 1989), and they are compounded by uncertainty as to what kind of economic and social system will eventually be established in the various countries, and what will be the influence in the region of the Soviet Union, a reunited Germany, and the European Community.

8 In this connection I also quoted the view of Wellmer (1971) that historical experience (of the many problems and failures of socialism) 'has thoroughly discredited all hopes of an economically grounded "mechanism" of emancipation'.

9 Britain constitutes a remarkable exception to the general course of European development, but this situation seems unlikely to persist. The attempt, during the past decade, to restore *laissez-faire* capitalism by subordinating economic activity and social provision to unregulated market forces, and returning to private ownership as much as possible of the nation's collective resources, has resulted in large-scale unemployment, increasing inequality, high inflation, a massive foreign trade deficit, a pitifully low rate of manufacturing investment, a deterioration

of public services, and a notable level of public squalor; in sum, a condition of general backwardness against which a substantial majority of the population now protests, supporting as an alternative an increase in public expenditure on social welfare, and also, to some extent, a return to public ownership in the sphere of essential services.

10   Which Marx (1844), be it noted, already saw as a central problem of the capitalist mode of production: the worker 'does not fulfil himself in his work, but denies himself, has a feeling of misery rather than well-being, does not develop freely his mental and physical powers but is physically exhausted and mentally debased . . . his work is not voluntary, but imposed, *forced labour*' and 'he feels himself at home only in his leisure time'.

11   See, for example, Durbin (1935), Pigou (1937), Dickinson (1939).

12   I have discussed the experience of planning more fully in Bottomore (1990, especially chs 3 and 4).

13   See the more extensive analysis of these problems in Bottomore (1990, ch. 8), and, on planning with markets, the valuable studies by Brus (1972), Horvat (1982), and most recently Brus and Laski (1989).

Bibliography

Abercrombie, Nicholas and Urry, John (1983), *Capital, Labour and the Middle Classes* (London: Allen & Unwin).

Adler, Max (1915), 'Zur Ideologie des Weltkrieges', *Der Kampf*, vol. 8.

Adler, Max (1933), 'Metamorphosis of the working class?' *Der Kampf*, vol. 26 (trans. in Bottomore and Goode, 1978).

Albertoni, Ettore A. (1987), *Mosca and the Theory of Élitism* (Oxford: Blackwell).

Andrieux, A. and Lignon, J. (1960), *L'Ouvrier d'aujourd'hui* (Paris: Marcel Rivière).

Aron, Raymond (1950), 'Social structure and the ruling class'; reprinted in *Power, Modernity and Sociology* (Aldershot: Edward Elgar, 1988).

Aron, Raymond (1964), *La Lutte de classes* (Paris: Gallimard).

Ash, Timothy Garton (1989), 'Does Central Europe exist?', in George Schöpflin and Nancy Wood (eds), *In Search of Central Europe* (Oxford: Polity Press/Blackwell).

Atkinson, A. B. (1974), *Unequal Shares: Wealth in Britain* (rev. edn, Harmondsworth: Penguin Books).

Avineri, Shlomo (1968), *The Social and Political Thought of Karl Marx* (Cambridge: Cambridge University Press).

Bahrdt, H. P. (1965), 'Contribution to discussion', in Otto Stammer (ed.), *Max Weber and die Soziologie heute* (Tübingen: J. C. B. Mohr), pp. 124–30.

Baltzell, E. Digby (1962), *An American Business Aristocracy* (New York: Collier Books).

Bauer, Otto (1907), *Die Nationalitätenfrage und die Sozialdemokratie* (2nd enlarged edn, Vienna: Wiener Volksbuchhandlung, 1924).

Bauer, Otto (1924), 'Voraussetzungen des Sozialismus', *Arbeiter-Zeitung*, 25 December.

Beard, Charles (1914), *Contemporary American History, 1877–1913* (New York: Macmillan).

Bechhofer, Frank and Elliott, Brian (eds) (1981), *The Petite Bourgeoisie: Comparative Studies of the Uneasy Stratum* (London: Macmillan).

Bednarik, K. (1953), *Der junge Arbeiter von heute – ein neuer Typ*

(Stuttgart: Gustav Kilpper Verlag. English trans. London: Faber & Faber, 1955).

Benton, Ted (1981), ' "Objective" interests and the sociology of power', *Sociology*, vol. 15, no. 2.

Bernstein, Eduard (1899), *Evolutionary Socialism* (New York: Schocken, 1961).

Beynon, Huw (1984), *Working for Ford* (2nd edn, Harmondsworth: Penguin Books).

Bloch, Marc (1961), *Feudal Society* (London: Routledge & Kegan Paul).

Booth, Charles (1891–1903), *Life and Labour of the People in London* (London: Macmillan).

Bottomore, Tom (1952), 'La Mobilité sociale dans la haute administration française', *Cahiers internationaux de sociologie*, vol. 13.

Bottomore, Tom (1964), *Élites and Society* (Harmondsworth: Penguin Books, 1966).

Bottomore, Tom (1967), *Critics of Society* (London: Allen & Unwin).

Bottomore, Tom (1975), *Sociology as Social Criticism* (London: Allen & Unwin).

Bottomore, Tom (1979), *Political Sociology* (London: Hutchinson).

Bottomore, Tom (ed.) (1983), *A Dictionary of Marxist Thought* (Oxford: Blackwell).

Bottomore, Tom (1984a), *The Frankfurt School* (London: Tavistock).

Bottomore, Tom (1984b), *Sociology and Socialism* (Brighton: Wheatsheaf).

Bottomore, Tom (1985), *Theories of Modern Capitalism* (London: Allen & Unwin).

Bottomore, Tom (1987), *Sociology: A Guide to Problems and Literature* (3rd edn, London: Allen & Unwin).

Bottomore, Tom (ed.) (1988), *Interpretations of Marx* (Oxford: Blackwell).

Bottomore, Tom (1990), *The Socialist Economy: Theory and Practice* (Hemel Hempstead: Harvester–Wheatsheaf).

Bottomore, Tom and Brym, Robert (eds) (1989), *The Capitalist Class: An International Study* (Hemel Hempstead: Harvester-Wheatsheaf).

Bottomore, Tom and Goode, Patrick (1978), *Austro-Marxism* (Oxford: Clarendon Press).

Braudel, Fernand (1972), *The Mediterranean* (2 vols, London: Collins).

Braverman, H. (1974), *Labour and Monopoly Capital* (New York: Monthly Review Press).

Broekmeyer, M. J. (ed.) (1970), *Yugoslav Workers' Self-Management* (Dordrecht: Reidel).

Brus, W. (1972), *The Market in a Socialist Economy* (London: Routledge & Kegan Paul).

Brus, W. and Laski, K. (1989), *From Marx to the Market* (Oxford: Clarendon Press).
Brym, Robert J. (1989), 'Canada', in Bottomore and Brym (1989).

Copeman, G. H. (1955), *Leaders of British Industry: A Study of the Careers of More than a Thousand Public Company Directors* (London: Gee & Co.).
Corey, Lewis (1935), *The Crisis of the Middle Class* (New York: Cevici Friede).
Croce, Benedetto (1913), *Historical Materialism and the Economics of Karl Marx* (London: Howard Latimer).
Cruse, Harold (1967), *The Crisis of the Negro Intellectual* (New York: William Morrow & Co.).

Dahrendorf, Ralf (1959), *Class and Class Conflict in an Industrial Society* (London: Routledge & Kegan Paul).
Dalton, Hugh (1920), *Some Aspects of the Inequality of Incomes in Modern Societies* (London: Routledge).
Davis, Kingsley and Moore, Wilbert E. (1945), 'Some principles of stratification', *American Sociological Review*, vol. 10, no. 2.
Dickinson, H. D. (1939), *Economics of Socialism* (London: Oxford University Press).
Disraeli, Benjamin (1845), *Sybil; or, The Two Nations* (Hughenden edn of the novels and tales, 11 vols, 1881).
Djilas, Milovan (1957), *The New Class* (London: Thames & Hudson).
Domhoff, G. W. (1983), *Who Rules America Now?* (Englewood Cliffs, NJ: Prentice-Hall).
Dumont, Louis (1970), *Homo Hierarchicus: The Caste System and its Implications* (London: Weidenfeld & Nicholson).
Durbin, E. F. M. (1935), 'The importance of planning'; reprinted in *Problems of Economic Planning* (London: Routledge & Kegan Paul, 1949).
Durkheim, Émile (1897), Review of A. Labriola, *Essais sur la conception matérialiste de l'histoire, Revue philosophique*.

Engels, Friedrich (1884), *The Origin of the Family, Private Property and the State* (New York: International Publishers, 1972).

Field, Frank (ed.) (1983), *The Wealth Report 2* (London: Routledge & Kegan Paul).
Finley, M. I. (ed.) (1968), *Slavery in Classical Antiquity* (Cambridge: Heffer).
Finley, M. I. (1983), 'Slavery', in Bottomore (1983).
Fraser, Ronald (ed.) (1968, 1969), *Work* (2 vols, Harmondsworth: Penguin Books in association with *New Left Review*).
Friedrich, C. J., Curtis, M. and Barber, B. R. (eds) (1969), *Totalitarianism in Perspective: Three Views* (London: Pall Mall).

Galbraith, J. K. (1958), *The Affluent Society* (Harmondsworth: Penguin Books, 1962).

Gallie, Duncan (1978), *In Search of the New Working Class* (Cambridge: Cambridge University Press).

Gay, Peter (1952), *The Dilemma of Democratic Socialism: Eduard Bernstein's Challenge to Marx* (London: Oxford University Press).

Gerth, Hans and Mills, C. Wright (eds) (1947), *From Max Weber: Essays in Sociology* (London: Kegan Paul, Trench, Trubner).

Giddens, Anthony (1973), *The Class Structure of the Advanced Societies* (London: Hutchinson).

Gilmour, Robin (1981), *The Idea of the Gentleman in the Victorian Novel* (London: Allen & Unwin).

Glass, D. V. (ed.) (1954), *Social Mobility in Britain* (London: Routledge & Kegan Paul).

Goldthorpe, J. H. (1980), *Social Mobility and Class Structure in Modern Britain* (Oxford: Clarendon Press).

Goldthorpe, John and Lockwood, David (1963), 'Affluence and the British class structure', *Sociological Review*, vol. 11, no. 2, pp. 133–63.

Golubović, Zagorka (1986), 'Yugoslav society and "socialism"', in Golubović and Stojanović, *The Crisis of the Yugoslav System* (Study no. 14 in the research project 'Crises in Soviet-type systems', Cologne: Index).

Gordey, Michel (1952), *Visa to Moscow* (London: Gollancz).

Gorz, André (1982), *Farewell to the Working Class: an Essay on Post-Industrial Socialism* (London: Pluto Press).

Gramsci, Antonio (1929–35), *Selections from the Prison Notebooks*, ed. Quintin Hoare and Geoffrey Nowell Smith (London: Lawrence & Wishart, 1971).

Habermas, Jürgen (1973), *Legitimation Crisis* (London: Heinemann, 1976).

Hare, Paul, Radice, Hugo and Swain, Nigel (1981), *Hungary: A Decade of Economic Reform* (London: Allen & Unwin).

Heath, Anthony (1981), *Social Mobility* (London: Fontana).

Hegedüs, András (1976), *Socialism and Bureaucracy* (London: Allison & Busby).

Hilferding, Rudolf (1910), *Finance Capital: A Study of the Latest Phase of Capitalist Development* (London: Routledge & Kegan Paul, 1981).

Hilferding, Rudolf (1940), 'State capitalism or totalitarian state economy', *Socialist Courier* (New York); reprinted in *Modern Review* (New York), vol. 1, 1947.

Hilferding, Rudolf (1941), *Das historische Problem*, unfinished manuscript; published in *Zeitschrift für Politik* (New Series, vol. 1, 1954).

118   *Classes in Modern Society*

Hilton, R. H. (1983), 'Feudal society', in Bottomore (1983).
Hindess, Barry (1971), *The Decline of Working Class Politics* (London: MacGibbon & Kee).
Hindess, Barry (1987), *Politics and Class Analysis* (Oxford: Blackwell).
Hindess, Barry (1988), *Choice, Rationality and Social Theory* (London: Unwin Hyman).
Hindess, Barry (1989), *Political Choice and Social Structure* (Aldershot: Edward Elgar).
Hobsbawm, Eric (1964), 'The labour aristocracy in nineteenth-century Britain', in *Labouring Men* (London: Weidenfeld & Nicholson).
Hofstadter, Richard (1963), 'The pseudo-conservative revolt' and 'Pseudo-conservatism revisited: a postscript', in Daniel Bell (ed.), *The Radical Right* (New York: Doubleday).
Horvat, Branko (1982), *The Political Economy of Socialism* (Oxford: Martin Robertson).

Jenkins, Roy (1952), 'Equality', in *New Fabian Essays*, ed. R. H. S. Crossman (London: Turnstile Press).
Johnson, Terence J. (1972), *Professions and Power* (London: Macmillan).

Kautsky, Karl (1927), *The Materialist Conception of History* (abridged trans., New Haven: Yale University Press, 1988).
Kelsall, R. K. (1955), *Higher Civil Servants in Britain from 1870 to the Present Day* (London: Routledge & Kegan Paul).
Klingender, F. D. (1935), *The Condition of Clerical Labour in Britain* (London: Martin Lawrence).
Kohn, H. (1967), *The Idea of Nationalism* (New York: Collier Books).
Kolakowski, Leszek (1978), *Main Currents of Marxism* (3 vols, Oxford: Clarendon Press).
Konrád, George (1990), article on Eastern Europe, *Guardian*, 14 April.
Konrád, George and Szelényi, Ivan (1979), *The Intellectuals on the Road to Class Power* (Brighton: Harvester).

Larrain, Jorge (1989), *Theories of Development* (Oxford: Polity Press/Blackwell).
Laslett, John H. M. and Lipset, Seymour M. (eds) (1974), *Failure of a Dream? Essays in the History of American Socialism* (Garden City, NY: Doubleday; rev. edn, Berkeley: University of California Press, 1984).
Lipset, Seymour M. and Bendix, Reinhard (1959), *Social Mobility in Industrial Society* (Berkeley and Los Angeles: University of California Press).
Lockwood, David (1958), *The Blackcoated Worker* (2nd edn with postscript. Oxford: Clarendon Press, 1989). (London: Allen & Unwin).

Machajski, Waclaw (1905), *The Intellectual Worker* (in Russian; summarized in Max Nomad, *Rebels and Renegades*, New York: Macmillan, 1932).

Maddison, Angus (1982), *Phases of Capitalist Development* (Oxford: Oxford University Press).

Mallet, Serge (1975), *The New Working Class* (Nottingham: Spokesman Books).

Mann, Michael (1973), *Consciousness and Action among the Western Working Class* (London: Macmillan).

Marceau, Jane (1989), *A Family Business? The Making of an International Business Élite* (Cambridge: Cambridge University Press).

Marcuse, Herbert (1964), *One-Dimensional Man: Studies in the Ideology of Advanced Industrial Society* (London: Routledge & Kegan Paul).

Marshall, Alfred (1873), 'The future of the working classes'; in A. C. Pigou (ed.), *Memorials of Alfred Marshall* (London: Macmillan, 1925).

Marshall, T. H. (1950), *Citizenship and Social Class and Other Essays* (Cambridge: Cambridge University Press).

Marx, Karl (1844), *Economic and Philosophical Manuscripts*.

Marx, Karl (1845), *The Holy Family*.

Marx, Karl (1847), *The Poverty of Philosophy*.

Marx, Karl (1848), *Wage-Labour and Capital*.

Marx, Karl (1852), 'The Chartists', *New York Daily Tribune*, 25 August.

Marx, Karl (1857–8), *Grundrisse*.

Marx, Karl (1859), *A Contribution to the Critique of Political Economy*.

Marx, Karl (1861–3), *Theories of Surplus Value* (ed. Karl Kautsky, Stuttgart: J. H. W. Dietz Nachf., vols 1 and 2, 1905; vol. 3, 1910).

Marx, Karl (1867, 1885, 1894) *Capital*, Vols. I, II and III.

Marx, Karl (1871), *The Civil War in France*.

Marx, Karl and Engels, Friedrich (1845–6), *The German Ideology*.

Marx, Karl and Engels, Friedrich (1848), *Communist Manifesto*.

Michels, Roberto (1911), *Political Parties* (Glencoe, Ill.: The Free Press, 1966).

Miliband, Ralph (1983), *Class Power and State Power* (London: Verso).

Miller, S. M. (1960), 'Comparative social mobility', *Current Sociology*, vol. 9, no. 1.

Miller, William (1962), 'American historians and the business élite', in William Miller (ed.), *Men in Business* (new edn, New York: Harper & Row).

Mills, C. Wright (1951), *White Collar: The American Middle Classes* (New York: Oxford University Press).

Mills, C. Wright (1956), *The Power Élite* (New York: Oxford University Press).

Mosca, Gaetano (1896), *The Ruling Class* (New York: McGraw-Hill, 1939).

O'Connor, Julia S. and Brym, Robert J. (1988), 'Public welfare expenditure in O.E.C.D. countries: towards a reconciliation of inconsistent findings', *British Journal of Sociology*, vol. 39.

Offe, Claus (1972), 'Political authority and class structures – an analysis of late capitalist societies', *International Journal of Sociology*, vol. 2, no. 1.

Ossowski, Stanislaw (1963), *Class Structure in the Social Consciousness* (London: Routledge & Kegan Paul).

Parkin, Frank (1968), *Middle Class Radicalism* (Manchester: Manchester University Press).

Parkin, Frank (1971), *Class Inequality and Political Order* (London: MacGibbon & Kee).

Pigou, A. C. (1937), *Socialism versus Capitalism* (London: Macmillan, 1960).

Pijl, Kees van der (1989), 'The international level', in Bottomore and Brym (1989).

Playford, Clive and Pond, Chris (1983), 'The right to be unequal: inequality in incomes', in Field (1983).

Pond, Chris (1983), 'Wealth and the two nations', in Field (1983).

Popitz, H. *et al.* (1957), *Das Gesellschaftsbild des Arbeiters* (Tübingen: J. C. B. Mohr).

Postan, M. M. (1967), *Economic History of Western Europe, 1945–64* (London: Methuen).

Poulantzas, Nicos (1968), *Political Power and Social Classes* (London: New Left Books, 1973).

Poulantzas, Nicos (1974), *Classes in Contemporary Capitalism* (London: New Left Books, 1975).

Przeworski, Adam (1977), 'Proletariat into a class: the process of class formation from Karl Kautsky's *The Class Struggle* to recent controversies', *Politics and Society*, vol. 7.

Renner, Karl (1917), *Marxismus, Krieg und Internationale* (Stuttgart: J. H. W. Dietz).

Renner, Karl (1953), *Wandlungen der modernen Gesellschaft. Zwei Abhandlungen über die Probleme der Nachkriegszeit* (Vienna: Wiener Volksbuchhandlung).

Richta, Radovan (ed.) (1969), *Civilization at the Crossroads* (White Plains, NY: International Arts and Sciences Press).

Roemer, John (1982), *A General Theory of Exploitation and Class* (Cambridge, Mass.: Harvard University Press).

Rousseau, Jean-Jacques (1755), *A Dissertation on the Origin and Foundation of the Inequality of Mankind* (London: Dent, Everyman's Library, 1952).

Routh, Guy (1980), *Occupation and Pay in Great Britain 1906–79* (London: Macmillan).

Rowntree, B. Seebohm (1901), *Poverty: A Study of Town Life* (London: Macmillan).

Rubinstein, W. D. (1987), *Élites and the Wealthy in Modern British History* (Brighton: Harvester Press).

Sampson, Anthony (1962), *Anatomy of Britain* (London: Hodder & Stoughton).

Sassoon, Anne Showstack (1983), 'Hegemony', in Bottomore (1983).

Scase, Richard (1977), *Social Democracy in Capitalist Society: Working Class Politics in Britain and Sweden* (London: Croom Helm).

Schumpeter, J. A. (1942), *Capitalism, Socialism and Democracy* (6th edn, London: Unwin Hyman, 1987).

Scott, Alan (1990), *Ideology and the New Social Movements* (London: Unwin Hyman).

Scott, John (1982), *The Upper Classes: Property and Privilege in Britain* (London: Macmillan).

Sombart, Werner (1906), *Why is there no Socialism in the United States?* (London: Macmillan, 1976).

Sorel, Georges (1895), 'Les Théories de M. Durkheim', *Le Devenir Social*, vol. 1, nos 1 and 2.

Spohn, Willfried and Bodemann, Y. Michal (1989), 'Federal Republic of Germany', in Bottomore and Brym (1989).

Srinivas, M. N. *et al.* (1959), 'Caste', *Current Sociology*, vol. 8, no. 3.

Stein, Lorenz von (1842), *The History of the Social Movement in France, 1789–1850* (3rd edn, 1850. Trans. of major sections, Totowa, NJ: Bedminster Press, 1964).

Stojanović, Svetozar (1973), *Between Ideals and Reality: A Critique of Socialism and its Future* (New York: Oxford University Press).

Széll, György (1988), 'Participation, workers' control and self-management', *Current Sociology*, vol. 36, no. 3.

Tawney, R. H. (1952), *Equality* (4th rev. edn, London: Allen & Unwin).

Terkel, Studs (1974), *Working* (rev. ed., Harmondsworth: Penguin Books, 1985).

Thomas, Hank and Logan, Chris (1982), *Mondragon: An Economic Analysis* (London: Allen & Uwin).

Tilly, Charles (ed.) (1975), *The Formation of National States in Western Europe* (Princeton, NJ: Princeton University Press).

Tocqueville, Alexis de (1835), *Democracy in America* (New York: Harper, 1966).

Touraine, Alain (1971), *The Post-Industrial Society* (New York: Random House).

Touraine, Alain (1977), *The Self-Production of Society* (Chicago: University of Chicago Press).

122   *Classes in Modern Society*

Touraine, Alain (1980), *L'Après-Socialisme* (Paris: Grasset).
Touraine, Alain (1981), *The Voice and the Eye: An Analysis of Social Movements* (Cambridge: Cambridge University Press).
Touraine, Alain (1987), 'The rise and fall of the French labour movement', in William Outhwaite and Michael Mulkay (eds), *Social Theory and Social Criticism* (Oxford: Blackwell).
Trollope, Anthony (1864), *Can You Forgive Her?* (Penguin edn, 1972; Oxford University Press World's Classics edn, 1982).
Trotsky, Leon (1937), *The Revolution Betrayed* (London: New Park, 1957).
Turner, Bryan S. (1983), 'Asiatic society', in Bottomore (1983).

Wall, Stephen (1972), Introduction to Penguin edition of Trollope's *Can You Forgive Her?*
Webb, Sidney (1931), 'Historic', in G. Bernard Shaw (ed.), *Fabian Essays in Socialism* (Reprint, London: The Fabian Society and Allen & Unwin).
Weber, Max (1918), 'Socialism'; in J. E. T. Eldridge (ed.), *Max Weber: The Interpretation of Social Reality* (London: Michael Joseph, 1970).
Weber, Max (1921), *Economy and Society* (3 vols, New York: Bedminster Press, 1968).
Weber, Max (1971), *Gesammelte politische Schriften* (3rd enlarged edn., Tübingen: J. C. B. Mohr).
Weinstein, James (1967), *The Decline of Socialism in America 1912–1925* (New York: Monthly Review Press).
Wellmer, Albrecht (1971), *Critical Theory of Society* (New York: Herder & Herder).
Weselowski, W. (1979), *Classes, Strata and Power* (London: Routledge & Kegan Paul).
Wiener, M. J. (1981), *English Culture and the Decline of the Industrial Spirit 1850–1980* (Cambridge: Cambridge University Press).
Wright, Erik Olin (1978), *Class, Crisis and the State* (London: New Left Books).
Wright, Erik Olin (1985), *Classes* (London: Verso).

Yanowitch, Murray (1963), 'The Soviet income revolution', *Slavic Review*, vol. 23, no. 4.

Zweig, F. (1961), *The Worker in an Affluent Society* (London: Heinemann).

Index